D0205726

TIPBOOK DRUMS

Tipbook
Drums

The Complete Guide

Hugo Pinksterboer

Tipbook
Drums

The Complete Guide

THE **TIPBOOK** COMPANY

The Best Guide To Your Instrument!

www.tipbook.com

Publishing details

This second edition published June 2007 by The Tipbook Company bv, The Netherlands.
Distribution for the USA by the Hal Leonard Corporation,
7777 West Bluemound Road, P.O. Box 13819, Milwaukee, Wisconsin 53213.
Typeset in Linotype Ergo and Minion.

Printed in the USA.

ISBN-13: 978-90-8767-102-0
ISBN-10: 90-8767-102-4

Thanks!

For their information, their expertise, their time, and their help we'd like to thank the following musicians, teachers, technicians and other experts:

Steve Clover, Andy Doerschuk (*Drum!*), Rick van Horn (*Modern Drummer*), Steve Smith, Cesar Zuiderwijk, Fred van Vloten, René Creemers, Ifor Baynes, Dennis Boxem and Erk Willemsen (*Slagwerkkrant*, the Dutch drummers' magazine), Pascale Jansen, Gabriel Laurens (EMD, Brussels), Robin Roetering, Gerrie Spaansen, Hans Waterman (*Music Maker*), Hans in 't Zand, Rob ter Maat, Piet Klaassen, and the people at Drumland.

The makers

Journalist, writer and musician **Hugo Pinksterboer**, author of The Tipbook Series has published hundreds of interviews, articles and instrument, DVD, CD, and book reviews for Dutch and international drummers' magazines. He is the author of the reference work for cymbals (*The Cymbal Book*, Hal Leonard).

Illustrator, designer, and musician **Gijs Bierenbroodspot** has worked as an art director for a wide variety of magazines and has developed numerous ad campaigns. While searching in vain for information about saxophone mouthpieces, he got the idea for this series of books on music and musical instruments. He is responsible for the layout and the illustrations for all of the Tipbooks.

Acknowledgements

Concept, design, and illustrations: Gijs Bierenbroodspot
Cover photo: René Vervloet
Editors: Robert L. Doerschuk and Michael J. Collins
Proofreaders: Nancy Bishop and René de Graaff

Anything missing?

Any omissions? Any areas that could be improved? Please go to www.tipbook.com to contact us, or send an email to info@tipbook.com. Thanks!

Contents

In brief

Have you just started to play the drums? Are you thinking about buying a drum set or cymbals? Or do you want to find out more about the instrument you already own? Then this book will tell you all you need to know, starting with the role of a drummer in a band before going on to the basics on the instrument, drum lessons and practicing, and what it all costs. But the main part of the book focuses on drums, cymbals, heads, sticks, hardware, tuning, the history of the drum set — and much more.

A good choice

Having read this book, you'll know enough to make a good choice when selecting drums, cymbals, sticks, or drum heads, and you'll be able to easily understand anything else you may want to read about these instruments, either in print or on the Internet.

Basics

If you have just started playing, or haven't yet begun, pay particular attention to the first four chapters. They explain the joy of drumming, the basic parts and elements of the drum set and their names, and they inform you on learning to play the drums, practicing, and buying or renting an instrument. This information also fully prepares you to read the rest of the book.

Advanced players

Advanced players can skip ahead to Chapter 5 where you will find

everything you need to know to make an informed purchase when you're going to buy a set of drums. Chapters 6, 7, 8, and 9 offer similar information on selecting and auditioning hardware, drum heads, sticks, and cymbals.

Tuning and maintenance

Everything to get the best out of your instrument can be found in Chapters 10 and 11, covering tuning, muffling, setting up the drums, maintenance, and related subjects.

Background information

The final chapters of this complete guide offer essential reading material on the history of the drum set, the family of the instrument, its production, and the main brand names that you'll come across.

US dollars

Please note that all prices mentioned in this book reflect only approximate street prices in US dollars.

Glossary

The glossary at the end of the book briefly explains most of the terms you'll come across as a drummer. Also included are an index of terms, and a couple of pages for essential notes on your equipment.

Rudiments and drum beats

Many readers of earlier editions of *Tipbook Drums* asked us to include basic rudiments, and drum beats for various styles of music. So we did — and you'll find all of this of on pages 189–225 of this new edition. Enjoy!

Hugo Pinksterboer

See and hear what you read with Tipcode

www.tipbook.com

In addition to the many illustrations on the following pages, Tipbooks offer you a new way to see — and hear! — what you are reading about. The Tipcodes that you will come across throughout this book give you access to short videos, sound files, and other additional information at www.tipbook.com.

Here is how it works: On page 119 of this book you can read about taking off a drum head using two drum keys simultaneously. Right above that paragraph it says **Tipcode DRUM-014**. Type in that code on the Tipcode page at www.tipbook.com and you will see a short video that shows you this technique.

TIPCODE

Tipcode Drum-014
You can loosen or tighten two tension rods at the same time, as shown in this Tipcode.

Enter code, watch video

You enter the Tipcode below the movie window on the Tipcode

page. In most cases, you'll see the relevant video and/or hear audio within five to ten seconds.

Tipcodes listed

For your convenience, the Tipcodes presented in this book are also listed on page 184.

Quick start

The vides and sound files are designed so that they start quickly. If you miss something the first time, you can of course repeat them. And if it all happens too fast, use the pause button below the movie window.

First, make your selection: Tipcode, chords and fingering charts, or the glossary.

The Tipcode window displays videos, fingering charts, chords, or a glossary of the terms used in this book.

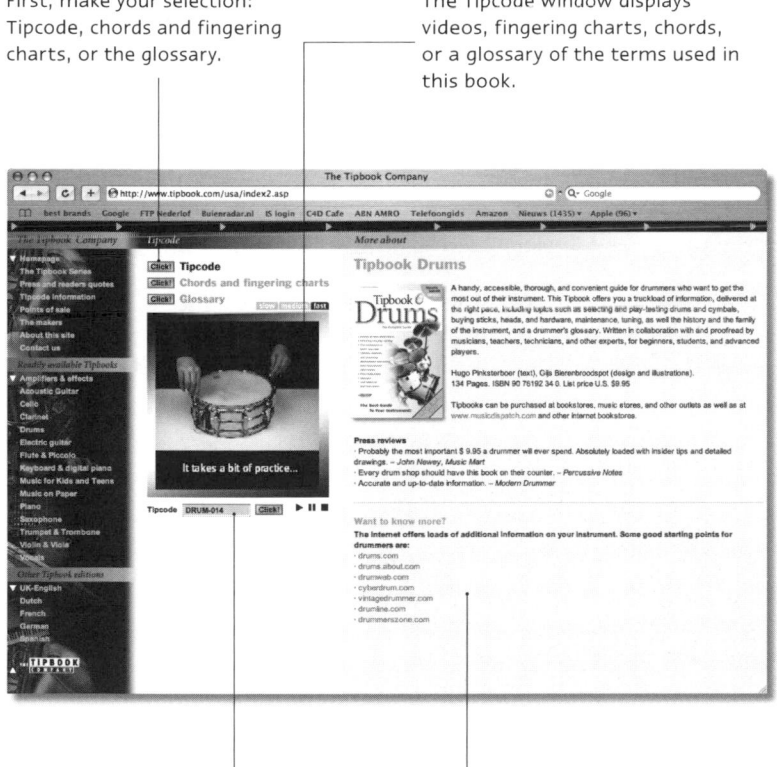

Enter a Tipcode here and click on the button. Want to see it again? Click again.

These links take you directly to other interesting sites.

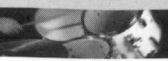

Software

If the software you need to view the videos is not yet installed on your computer, you'll automatically be told which software you need, and where you can download it. This software is free. Questions? Check out 'About this site' at www.tipbook.com.

Still more at www.tipbook.com

You can find even more information at www.tipbook.com. For instance, you can look up words in the glossaries of all the Tipbooks published to date. There are chord diagrams for guitarists and pianists; fingering charts for saxophonists, clarinetists, and flutists; and rudiments for drummers. Also included are links to most of the websites mentioned in the *Want to Know More?* section of each Tipbook.

1

A drummer?

You hear some pretty wild stories about drummers. They're savages who hit everything in sight. They always play as loud as they can. They can't read (music, that is). And then there's the one about the four-piece band; that's a band made up of three musicians and a drummer...

It's all jealousy, really. Every musician knows that the drummer is the most important member of the band. No band will sound great if there's a lousy drummer up there, and pretty much any band with a great drummer will sound at least acceptable. The drummer is the engine of the band. If your engine's not running okay, you won't get there. It's as simple as that.

Groove
Whether you're into country music, jazz, grunge, soul, funk, R&B or heavy metal, it's always the drummer who gets everyone to start and stop at the same time, who makes sure that nobody speeds up or slows down. Who reminds the singer to come in. Who makes it swing. Who makes it groove. Who makes it feel good.

All musical styles
As a drummer, you can play a wide variety of musical styles. You can play in bands where you need loads of amplification in order to make yourself heard, or in groups where you'll need to play as softly as you can, so the audience can still hear what the unamplified pianist is doing. You can play in big bands or trios, you can play improvised music or music that's written down note for note — and much more.

Easy to learn
One of the great things about drumming is that it's quite easy to learn. You may be able to play a couple of basic rock beats within two or three weeks — or even sooner — and you'll probably be able to play along to most of the songs in the charts within a couple of months. In the end, however, the drum set is just as hard to master as any other instrument.

Create your own
Almost every guitar has six strings. Every trumpet has three valves. Every piano looks basically the same. As a drummer, however, you can create your own instrument. You decide how many drums you use, you decide what sizes they have, and how you tune them. You also decide how many cymbals you use, and what sizes they have. In other words: the drum set is a very personal instrument.

(No) sound

A drum set is about the loudest instrument there is — and yet you can learn how to play the drums without making too much noise. For example, there are special practice sets, you can do all kinds of exercises on pillows, you can play your thighs with your hands, or… More on this is in Chapter 3.

2

A quick tour

A drum set is a set of drums, of course, as well as a set of cymbals, and a bunch of stands and pedals, collectively known as the hardware. This chapter introduces you to the main elements of the basic five-piece drum set — which happens to consist of at least ten or more pieces...

Many drummers use a five-piece drum set, 'five' referring to the number of drums in the set. The two main drums are the high-pitched, short and crisp sounding *snare drum* and the low-tuned *bass drum*. The other three are the toms: two on the bass drum, and one on the floor. Sounds familiar? Then just skip this chapter.

Tipcode Drum-001
This Tipcode shows you the main elements of a five-piece drum set plus cymbals.

Cymbals
Besides those drums, a drum set has various cymbals. The biggest cymbal is the *ride cymbal*, which you use to play the rhythm or ride. Alternatively, you can play the rhythm on the *hi-hat cymbals*: This is a pair of cymbals, one mounted above the other. You can play the hi-hats either by closing them via a pedal or by playing the top cymbal with your sticks. For accents, you use a smaller, thinner type of cymbal: the *crash cymbal*.

Stands and pedals
Ride and crash cymbals are mounted on cymbal stands, and there is a special type of stand for the snare drum. The two small toms are usually mounted on a tom holder, which in turn is mounted on the bass drum. The bass drum is played with a pedal, as is the hi-hat.

The shell
The main part of a drum is called the *shell*. This is the sound box of the drum. Snare drums often have metal shells; other drums usually have wooden shells.

6

crash cymbal — cymbal stand — ride cymbal

hi-hat cymbals

toms

hi-hat pedal

Five-piece set with ride, crash, and hi-hat cymbals.

snare drum —
snare drum stand —

bass drum —
bass drum pedal —

floor tom

As big as you like

You can make a drum set as big as you like. Many drummers use one or two extra toms, for instance. Some have two bass drums. And most drummers use additional cymbals: two or three crashes, for instance, one on the left and one on the right, or extra smaller or bigger cymbals. Chapter 16 shows some examples of drum sets, from a four-piece jazz set to a nine-piece rock set.

7

The heads

Most drums come with two heads. The *batter head* is the head that you play. Underneath is the bottom head, also known as the *resonant head*. If you take it off, you can clearly hear that the drum sounds less resonant; the tone is shorter and not as 'full'.

Rods and hoops

The drum head is held in place by a metal or wooden *counter hoop*. This hoop sits on the drum head's *flesh hoop*. Tightening the tension rods of a drum makes the counter hoop move down, pulling the head tight over the drum shell. The greater the head's tension, the higher the pitch of the drum will be.

The main parts of a drum.

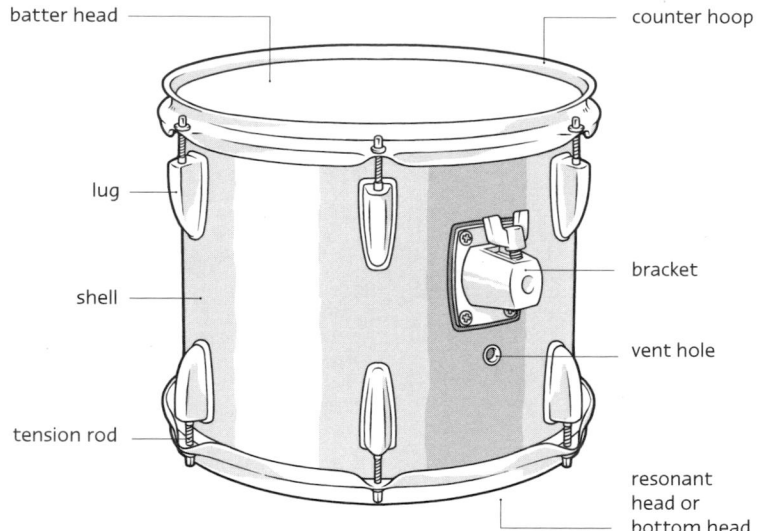

batter head — counter hoop
lug
shell
bracket
vent hole
tension rod
resonant head or bottom head

Vent hole

A small *vent hole*, often located in the center of the drum's badge, allows the air to move in and out of the drum. Hold you hand an inch away from the hole, play the drum, and you will feel the air move out as the stick hits the head.

The main drums

You can play probably ninety percent of all the songs in the charts with just a bass drum, a snare drum, and a pair of hi-hat cymbals.

8

The bass drum and the snare drum provide the heartbeat of the music in many styles, with the bass drum playing every downbeat (one and three), the snare drum every upbeat (two and four): boom, crack, boom, crack… The other drums and cymbals are basically there for embellishment; to play a fill or a break between two parts of a song, to play a solo, to spice up the basic beat, to create accents…

The bass drum

Because it is played with a pedal, the bass drum is also known as the *kick drum*. It has a low, deep, heavy, and fairly short sound. One of the most popular sizes is a 16x22 bass drum. The first figure refers to the shell depth; the second to its diameter, which equals the drum head size: A 16x22 bass drum requires a 22" bass drum head.

Spurs

Spurs on either side of the bass drum keep the instrument from rolling over or creeping away from you.

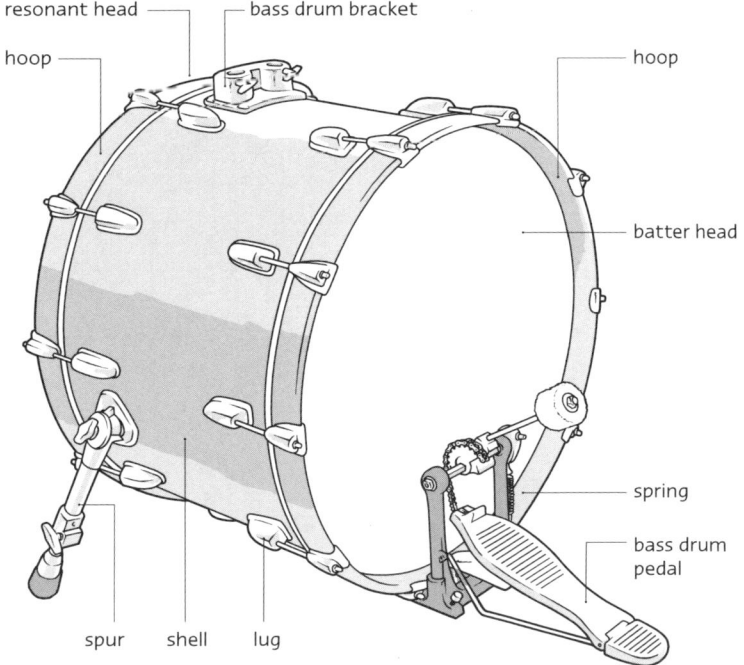

resonant head — bass drum bracket

hoop — hoop

batter head

spring

bass drum pedal

spur   shell   lug

A 16x22 bass drum with bass drum pedal.

9

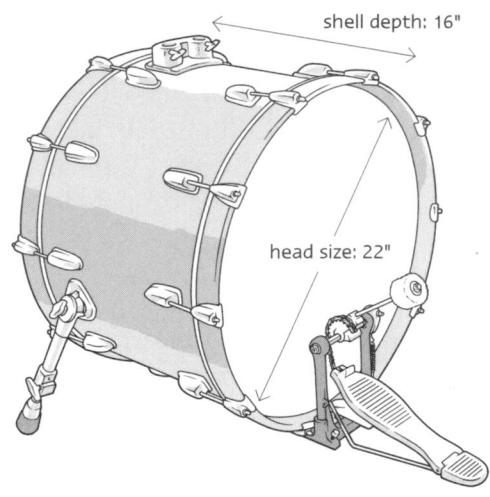

shell depth: 16"

head size: 22"

The snare drum

Both the sound and the name of the snare drum come from its set of *snares* or *snappy snares*: some twenty spiraled metal strands that rest against the bottom head. Every time you hit the drum, the snares bounce off and immediately snap back to the bottom head, producing a crisp, tight 'snare' sound. Most snare

The main parts of a snare drum.

lugs shell snare tension snare strainer

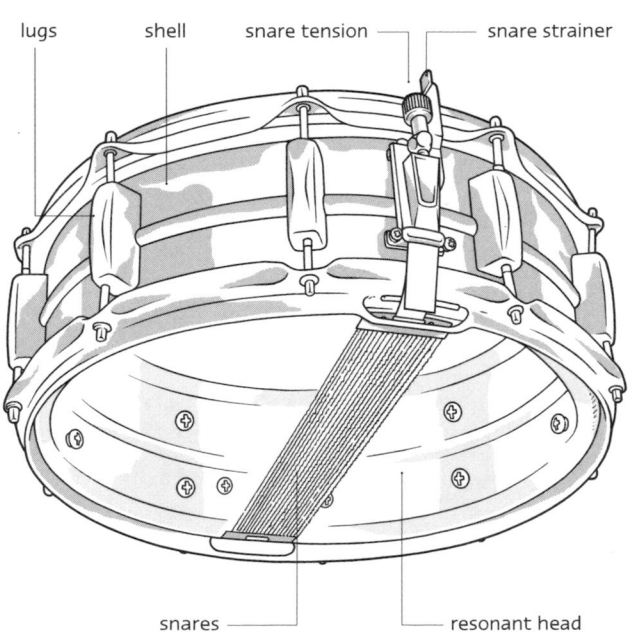

snares resonant head

drums are 14" in diameter, their depth varying from 4" to 6.5". A deeper drum will give a deeper sound.

Snare strainer

A knurled knob on the snare strainer allows you to vary the tension on the snares, making the sound a bit tighter or looser. You can use the handle of this mechanism to disengage the snares altogether. Without the snares, the drum sounds more like a high-pitched tom.

Toms

The toms, or tom-toms, are used mainly for rolls, fills, and solos. They come in a wide variety of sizes. The bigger a drum is, the lower it can sound. A typical five-piece set has two smaller toms, a 12" and a 13", mounted directly on the bass drum. They're also known as *rack toms*, *mounted toms*, or *hanging toms*. The third tom is the floor tom, usually a 16". It stands on its own, next to the snare drum.

Fusion

One of the main variations on this set is known as a *fusion set*. A fusion set usually has 10" and 12" toms, a stand-mounted 'hanging' 14" tom, and a 20" or 22" bass drum.

Power toms

Rack toms come in various depths. Traditionally, a 12" tom is 8" deep (8x12). *Power toms* are usually two inches deeper (10x12),

Head first

Drums are usually identified by their head size only: A 12" drum is a drum with a 12" diameter head. If they do specify the depth as well, most American drummers will state shell depth first. European drummers do it the other way around. In other words, an 'American' 10x12 tom equals a 'European' 12x10 tom. A basic rule avoids confusion: The higher number typically refers to the head size.

11

and there are also in-between sizes. The deeper a tom is, the deeper its sound will be. Most floor toms have *square sizes*, such as 16x16.

CYMBALS

A basic cymbal set consists of a ride cymbal, a pair of hi-hats and a crash cymbal. The hi-hat cymbals are played with your (left) foot, by closing them with the pedal, with sticks or, frequently, a combination of the two.

Keeping time
If you play a basic rock rhythm, you'll play a pattern of beats either on the ride cymbal or on the closed hi-hat cymbals. In other words, you *keep time* on the ride or on the hi-hats. The latter produce a tighter, more defined sound. If you want to hear a more open, sustained type of sound, you may want to use the ride cymbal.

Sizes
Most drummers go for a 20" ride, with the 22" also being quite popular. Other sizes are quite rare. The vast majority of drummers go for 14" hi-hat cymbals, though some prefer a 13" set.

Crashes
Crash cymbals, like toms, are named after the sound they make. And crash cymbals, like toms, are mainly used for adding color to the basic rhythm. They are thinner and smaller than ride cymbals, and respond very quickly, enabling a wide array of accents. If you only have one crash cymbal, it'll usually be a 16" or an 18". If you can afford two, a common choice would be one of each — but there are many other sizes available as well.

Effect cymbals
Besides rides, crashes and hi-hats, there are many other cymbal types, often referred to as *effect cymbals*, from paper-thin *splashes*

to raw and exotic sounding *China types* or Chinese cymbals. Read more about them in Chapter 9.

Bow, cup and edge

The *bow* of the cymbal is where you hit it when playing a ride pattern. The *cup* or *bell*, in the middle, can be used for tighter-sounding, penetrating accents or patterns. Crashes are played on the edge, with a glancing motion.

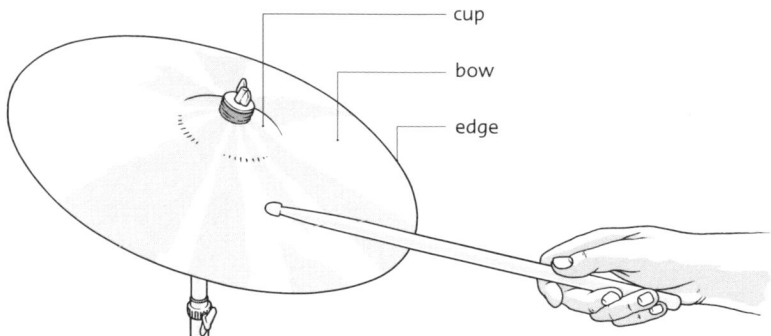

cup

bow

edge

The 'parts' of a cymbal.

Anything else

Along with all these cymbals, you can add a variety of other instruments to your set, ranging from timbales or the ever popular cowbells (see pages 148 and 152) to tambourines and other small percussion instruments. Chapter 16 shows some examples of drum sets.

STANDS AND PEDALS

The stands and pedals are collectively known as the *hardware*.

Straight stands and boom stands

Cymbal stands are usually made up of three telescoping tubes. The *tilter*, on top, allows you to angle the cymbal towards you. With the extra arm of a *boom stand* you can position a cymbal

13

pretty much anywhere you like. There are also special boom
stands for mounting toms.

Snare drum stand

The snare drum is set between the three arms of the so-called
basket of the snare drum stand. The *basket* is adjustable to the
exact size of the snare drum, and it can be tilted, too.

*A double-braced
hi-hat pedal
and snare drum
stand.*

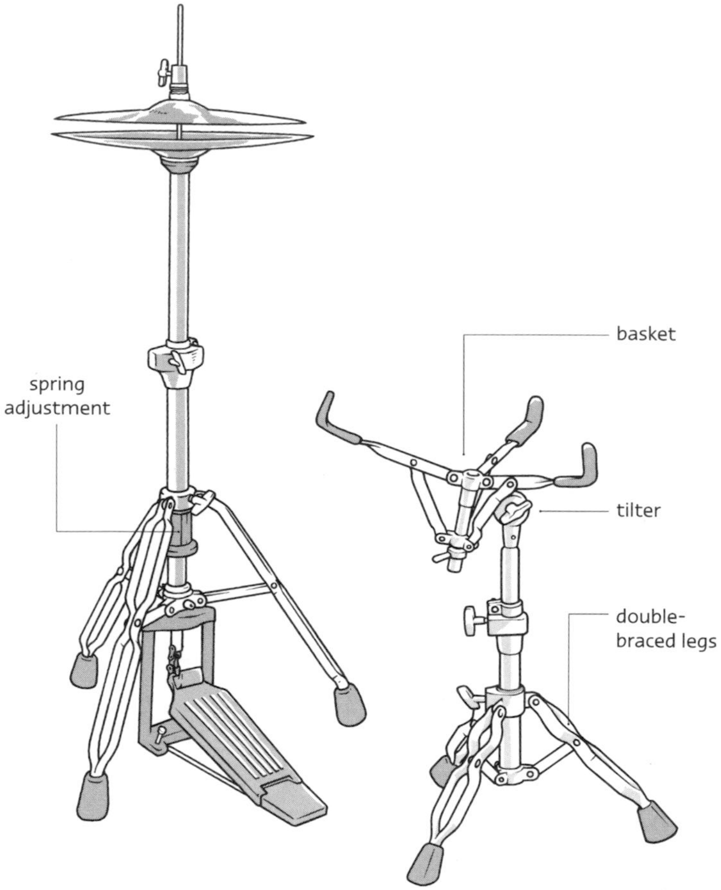

basket

spring
adjustment

tilter

double-
braced legs

The pedals

There is a wide variety of bass drum and hi-hat pedals around;
some very basic, others with very sophisticated ways to fully
adjust them to your liking. One of the most important and
common pedal adjustments is the *spring tension*, which allows

14

you to make the pedal feel lighter or heavier. The adjustable spring of a bass drum pedal is shown in the illustration on page 69. The hi-hat pedal spring is usually hidden inside the lower tube.

Left or right-handed?

If you're right-handed, you will probably arrange your set somewhat like the one illustrated in the beginning of this chapter. Left-handed drummers often set up the other way around, playing the bass drum with their left foot and the hi-hat with their right (see pages 141-142). Setting up this way is not the only option for left-handed drummers; other alternatives are given in Chapter 11, Setting up and maintenance.

15

3

Learning to play

Is it hard to learn to play the drums? Do you have to be able to read music? And what about practicing?

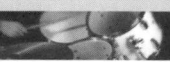

Many drummers are self-taught; they got themselves a drum set, figured out a basic beat and went on from there. Others started out playing just a snare drum for the first year or two, or a practice pad: After all, how can you play five drums if you can't play one? Both ways can be productive.

A teacher
There are many good drummers, and even some great ones, who are completely self-taught. Yet most of the world's top drummers have consulted a teacher at one time or another, rather than trying to work everything out for themselves.

What is there to learn?
Good drumming lessons are about more than knocking out beats. They also include subjects like stick technique, posture, rudiments, dynamics, keeping time, reading music, tuning, and an introduction to different styles of music. Most important, a good teacher will teach you to play music, instead of 'just' playing the drums.

School band
Many drummers have their first music lessons at school, and many of them started their drumming careers in the school's marching band or concert band.

Finding a teacher
Looking for a private teacher? Larger music stores may have teachers on staff, or they can refer you to one, and some players have found great teachers in musicians they have seen in performance. The Internet is another great resource as well (see page 187). You can also consult your local Musicians' Union, the band director at a high school in your vicinity, or check the classified ads in newspapers, in music magazines or on supermarket bulletin boards. Professional private teachers will usually charge between twenty-five and fifty dollars per hour. Some make house calls, for which you'll pay extra.

Collectives
You also may want to check whether there are any teachers'

18

collectives or community music schools in your vicinity. These collectives may offer extras such as ensemble playing, master classes, and clinics, in a wide variety of styles and at various levels.

First questions

On your first visit to a teacher, don't simply ask how much it costs. Here are a few tips to help you find out whether this is the person you're looking for.

- An **introductory lesson** allows you to see whether it clicks between you and the teacher — or, for that matter, between you and the drums. Asking to sit in on another student's lesson is an alternative.

- Is this teacher still interested in taking you on if you are just playing the drums **for the fun of it**, or are you supposed to practice at least three hours a day?

- Are you expected to make a large investment in **method books**, or are course materials provided?

- Can you **record your lessons**, so that you can listen to how you sounded when you get home?

- Is this teacher going to make you **practice rudiments** for two years, or will you be pushed onto a stage to play with a band as soon as possible?

Junior

You can pretty much start learning to play the drums as soon as you can walk, the only problem being that a regular drum set will be too big. There are special affordable junior sets for sale. If a child is serious about playing the drums, he or she should get a real drum set, rather than a toy drum set — so do consider visiting a real drum shop for such a purchase. A child may soon be big enough to play a regular drum set with a smaller (18") bass drum. Unfortunately, drum sets with bass drums in this size are not very common in the lower price ranges.

19

- There is much more on finding the perfect teacher in *Tipbook Music for Kids and Teens* (see page 235).

READING MUSIC

Have you ever seen a drummer reading music onstage? Probably not. Yet many of them can read music, and it's not hard to learn. The theory book in this series, *Tipbook Music on Paper — Basic Theory*, teaches you how in a handful of chapters (see page 231).

Five lines

Drum music is written in a similar way to music for other instruments, on the same staff. The main difference is that the position of the notes on the staff does not indicate a certain pitch, but a certain part of the drum set: Every part of the set has its own position on or between the five lines. Another difference: The cymbals are indicated by crosses (x). Here's what a basic rock beat looks like. There are more drum beats on pages 189–225.

TIPCODE

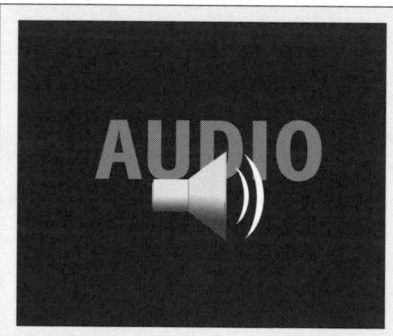

Tipcode DRUM-002
Play this Tipcode to hear what the rhythm below sounds like.

A basic rock rhythm

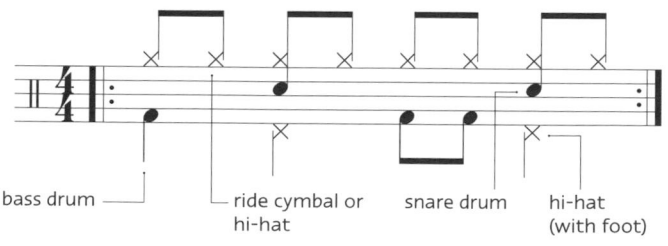

bass drum — ride cymbal or hi-hat — snare drum — hi-hat (with foot)

Why read?

Why would you learn to read music if you're a drummer?

- The #1 reason is so that you can instantly **play new music** and communicate with other musicians that you may have never played with before.

- If you can read, there are **tons of books** you can benefit from. Books with great ideas for grooves, fills and solos, books with effective exercises, books in which your favorite drummers show you how they did it, and so on.

- If you can read music, you can also **write music**. If you hear or figure out a good beat or a great fill, writing it down is easier and more reliable than remembering it.

- You **won't be lost** if somebody asks you to play sixteenths instead of eighths.

- Reading music makes you **more of a musician**, on top of being a drummer.

PRACTICING

Drumming makes a lot of noise. What to do about it when you're practicing? And while you're at it, how long should you practice, and what about metronomes and drum computers?

Half an hour

Many top drummers spent up to four or eight hours a day practicing, over several years — or more. If you can't spare that much time, you can make appreciable progress at half an hour per day. The more often you practice, the faster you learn. As with any other instrument, you're better off practicing, say, half an hour a day rather than a couple of hours once a week.

Less noise

There are four basic solutions to reduce the amount of sound you're bound to produce. Reduce the volume of your instrument,

21

replace your drums with something less noisy, prevent the noise from getting out or, if all else fails, do your practicing someplace else.

Agreed practice times
Lots of musicians keep neighbors and family happy simply by agreeing to fixed practice times.

Muffling your instrument
Stuffing your drums with blankets or cushions will quiet them down, but it takes hours to turn the set into a playable musical instrument again. What's more, even when it's stuffed completely, the bass drum is still bound to transmit a fair amount of annoyance through floors and walls (contact noise!).

Discs and bands
A much more flexible solution is to use a series of special muffling discs that you put on the batter heads of your drums. There are similar designs for bass drums and cymbals as well. A drawback of these discs is that they alter the way your instrument feels. The rebound of your sticks will be strongly reduced, depending on the exact hardness of the pad's material. Your cymbals will keep feeling more like cymbals if you muffle them with a wide elastic band. There are commercially available bands made to fit most cymbal sizes.

Mesh heads
You can also replace your regular drumheads with a set of *mesh heads*, which feature a very strong type of gauze, instead of the usual plastic film. These noiseless heads, which are also used on some types of electronic drums, offer a rebound that is quite similar to that of regular drum heads.

Pillows and pads
Unlike other musicians, drummers have a wide choice of alternatives for their 'real' instrument. Playing pillows, for one, has proven to be very effective for many drummers, though there are many teachers who thoroughly dislike the idea. Slightly noisier, but less dusty, is the *practice pad*, either a single pad or

a number of them, set up as a drum set. Practice pads come in two basic varieties: Some have a ply of soft or hard rubber which you play on. Others have a tunable drum head with foam rubber underneath. For snare drum practicing, practice pads with a 'snare' sound are available as well.

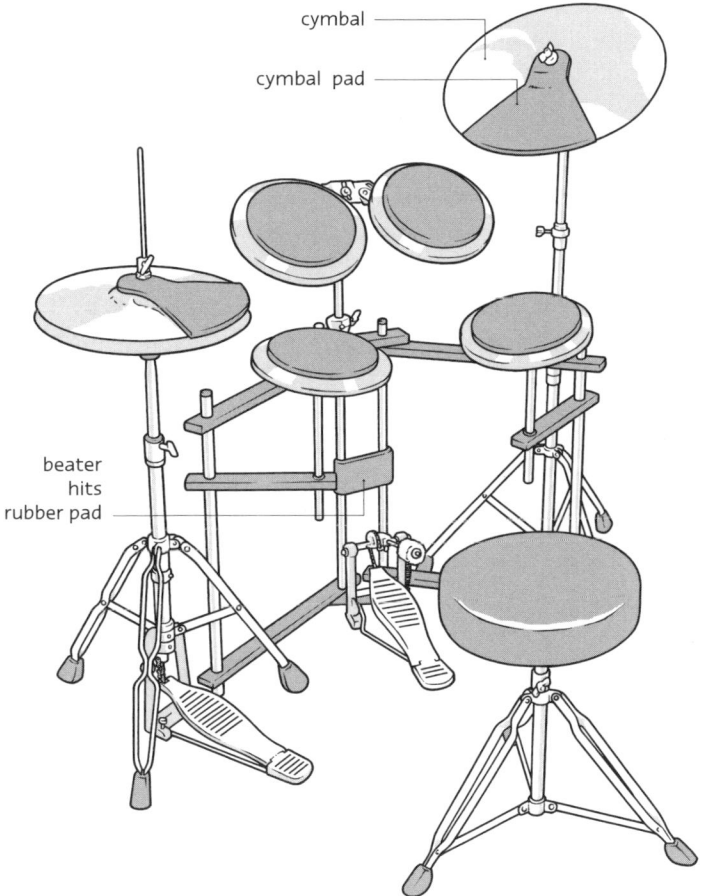

cymbal

cymbal pad

beater
hits
rubber pad

A practice set.

Fast rebound

Pretty much all these practice pads produce is the sound of your stick hitting the surface. Most of them have a faster rebound than real drums do — so when you switch back to real drums, they tend to feel slower. Mesh drum heads feel more like real drum heads.

23

Practice pedals

Also available are noiseless practice pedals for your feet, introduced by The Hansenfütz company.

TIP

> # Electronic drums
>
> _Practice pads don't sound like drums at all. Electronic drums do. Electronic drum sets usually consist of a series of pads or shallow drums with mesh heads which have built-in triggers. These triggers convert your playing to electronic signals which are fed to a sound module (see pages 153–154), programmed with numerous digital drum sounds. The end result can be very close (or even very, very close) to the real thing. They're great for practicing; simply plug in a set of headphones! Roland and Yamaha are the leading brands in electronic drums. Dedicated drum amplifiers are quite rare; onstage, electronic drums are usually hooked up to the PA._

Soundproofing

Practicing on a muffled instrument or on pads allows you to work on technique and timing, but it'll hardly help in developing your sound. If you want to practice on the same instrument you play on stage, soundproofing a room is an option. The costs vary greatly, depending on how much you want or need to reduce the sound by, for instance. Making a room really soundproof easily costs thousands of dollars. There are various books available on the subject, you can ask around to find people who have soundproofed a room, or you can hire a specialized contractor to do the job.

Prefab

As an alternative, you can get yourself a prefab sound-reducing cubicle, available in a variety of makes and sizes. They're easily as expensive as soundproofing a room to the same effect, but you can take them along if you move.

Practicing elsewhere

24

In most cities there are practice studios or rehearsal rooms that

you can rent by the hour — with a band, but also on your own, of course. Many practice studios come with a drum set, which also may include a set of cymbals, so all you need to bring with you are your sticks. Rental costs are usually quite reasonable. To keep them down even more, you could consider renting a room once a week and using a practice set for the rest of the week.

More
Additional tips on practicing can be found in *Tipbook Music for Kids and Teens* (see page 235).

YOUR OWN EARS

Drumming can be harmful to your ears. Even practicing as little as fifteen minutes a day may cause permanent damage. As hearing loss or damage is usually noticed only when it's too late, prevention is the key.

Cheap or expensive...
The cheapest foam plastic earplugs, available from most music stores and drugstores, will make the band sound as if they're not in the same room with you anymore. The most expensive earplugs, which are custom-made to fit your ears, usually have adjustable or replaceable filters which reduce the volume without affecting the sound.

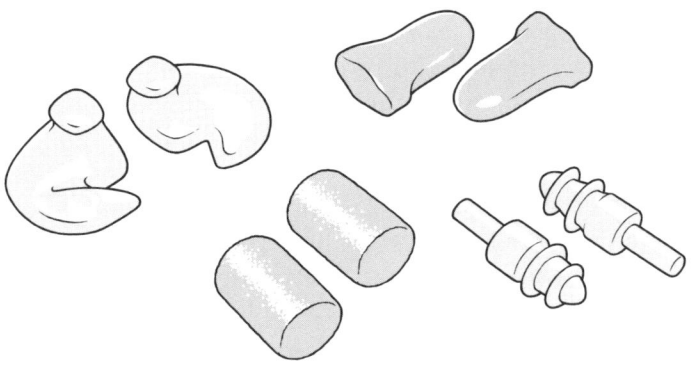

Some affordable types of ear plugs.

25

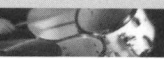
... and in between

Ear muffs may work well if you don't like to stick things into your ear. Plastic earplugs vary in their sound-reducing effects, as well as in how easy they are to clean. Ask fellow drummers and band members for their experiences, and don't hesitate to try a few until you find the ones that really fit and work for you. A hearing aid will cost more in the long run, ringing ears (*tinnitus*) never stop ringing, and hearing loss is often irreversible.

DRUM MACHINES, DVDS, AND MORE

You can buy all kinds of things to make practicing more efficient, more fun, or even both.

Keeping time

Drummers are supposed to keep time, and to keep the band from speeding up or slowing down. Some drummers have a sense of tempo that makes their time as steady as can be, at every tempo. Most drummers don't. That's where metronomes come in. These small electronic or mechanical devices click or bleep in a steady tempo that you set yourself.

Loud?

A metronome doesn't have to be really loud in order to be heard. As soon as you're a bit off, your hit will not coincide with the metronome's beat; you'll hear the metronome beat, and that'll tell you you're off. Don't go for one that you can hardly hear at all, however. Rather buy one with an adjustable volume level instead. Pretty much every metronome comes with an LED that blinks to indicate the beat, so you have visual control too.

Special metronomes

There are also special metronomes for drummers, with a variety of built-in sounds, and even with programming facilities, allowing you to store the tempos of a number of songs. These metronomes can also play at higher volume levels.

A special drummer's metronome, programmable, with extra power and various sounds (Tama).

Drum machine

As an alternative you can use a drum machine. They're more expensive of course, but they 're more flexible too, they have more sounds (programmable bass patterns, for example), and so they're nicer to work with. Phrase trainers are great practice devices too; they can slow down a musical phrase from CD, for example, enabling you to figure out even the meanest, fastest licks at your own tempo. There is computer software available that does the same thing.

Books, DVDs, and CDs

There's a lot you can learn from books, DVDs, and CDs.

- **Drum books** come in many types and formats, for drummers at every level. Quite a lot of them include a CD with examples or play-along exercises. Drummers' magazines offer practice material too.

- There are loads of **drum DVDs**, most of them made by well-known drummers who show you their tricks of the trade. These DVDs usually last anywhere from thirty to ninety minutes.

27

Booklets with printouts of the recorded rhythms and exercises are not always included.

- **Regular CDs** are great for practicing. Play a CD of your favorite band, put on a pair of headphones, get behind your set, and go. Thousands of drummers have done it that way. Practicing rudiments, either on a real drum or on something less noisy, can be a lot more fun if you do that to music too.

Record yourself
It's hard to really listen to yourself while you're playing. That's why many musicians record their practice sessions. A portable recording device (*e.g.*, walkman, minidisc recorder) with a built-in microphone is basically all you need, but you'll get more enjoyable and instructive recordings if you use better equipment.

And finally
Two great ways to learn how to play? One, play as much as you can. Alone, or in a band. Two, go out to see other musicians play. Living legends or local amateurs, every gig's a learning experience.

4

Buying drums

You can get yourself a new five-piece drum set with cymbals and a throne for as little as five or six hundred dollars. Want to start out even cheaper? Then buy secondhand, or just get a snare drum or a practice pad and a pair of sticks. This chapter tells you what you should know before you go out shopping. What to pay attention to once you're in the store you'll find in Chapters 5 and beyond.

A brand new five-piece drum set may cost anywhere between about four hundred and four thousand dollars, or even more. What's in between those extremes?

For gigging

A decent drum set and a decent set of cymbals, good enough to be played at a proper gig, will set you back somewhere between a thousand and fifteen hundred dollars. From that point on, things can only get better — and more expensive.

Comparing prices

When comparing drum set prices, take a good look at what you're going to get for your money. The cheapest sets often come with cymbals, but most are offered without. Similarly, the more you pay, the less (!) chance there is that hardware will be included. Drum sets without hardware are usually referred to as *shell sets* — which, in turn, may come with or without a snare drum.

Hardware

A basic hardware set usually has bass drum and hi-hat pedals, a snare stand, and a straight cymbal stand. Sometimes a second (boom) stand is included, too, or even a throne. Some manufacturers offer pre-packed hardware sets. Prices start at about two hundred dollars.

Better

The differences between a decent starter's set and top-of-the-range professional equipment have become harder and harder to spot in recent years. So why spend extra money on an expensive set?

A 'richer' sound

A more expensive set should produce a 'more expensive' sound — a 'richer' sound, you might say, with punchier lows and brighter highs, more color and carrying power. These results derive from the features that come with a higher price: selected woods for the shells, better workmanship, more research & development, original designs rather than copies, and hardware that's sturdier, easier to adjust, and better looking. And of course, if you're really

30

prepared to fork out a lot of money, part of what you pay will be for status or exclusivity, too.

More to choose from

Paying more also usually means there are more colors and drum sizes (shell diameters, depths, thicknesses…) to choose from. Low-budget series are often only available in two or three colors and in the basic five-piece setup — so you can't add matching toms later on.

The heads

One technique used by manufacturers to keep the price of entry-level sets down is to use inexpensive, low-quality heads, which won't allow the drums to sound as good as they can. Fortunately, it won't cost you too much to replace them with a set of good, professional quality batter heads (see Chapter 7).

CYMBALS

You can get yourself a ride, a crash, and a pair of hi-hat cymbals for as little as a two hundred dollars — but don't expect them to sound very pleasing. If you want professional cymbals, be prepared to pay ten times that amount or more. A set of intermediate cymbals, good enough to get you through a proper gig, will often set you back some five hundred dollars.

Nothing you can do

There's a vital difference between drums and cymbals. Pretty much every drum set can be made to sound at least decent, with some good heads and some good tuning. If a cheap cymbal sounds cheap, however, there's nothing you can do about it.

The other way around

A tip: Shop around for cymbals first, and see how much that leaves

31

you for a drum set. Most beginning drummers do it the other way around — but low-budget cymbals are more likely to offend your ears than low-budget drums ever will.

DRUM HEADS AND STICKS

How often you have to change heads and how long it takes to break a stick largely depends on how hard you play, but also on the sound you're after. If you happen to like the crisp sound of a new snare drum batter head, you'll have to replace it long before it has worn out to a point where you can't play it anymore.

An hour or a year
Some heavy-hitting pro drummers replace the batter heads of their snare drums every night, and the batter heads of their tom toms every third night. There are also pro drummers who use the same batter heads for over a year. And sticks? Some drummers (definitely not just pros) go through three pairs a night, while others use the same pair for months.

In between
If you play, say, six to eight hours a week and you don't play really loud, the batter heads on your toms and bass drum may last six months or more before they start losing their sound. Snare drum batters go quicker, after perhaps one or two months, simply because this is the drum you hit most often. Resonant heads can stay on much longer — basically until they're stretched (see page 118). If you're not an aggressive drummer, a pair of sticks will last you at least a month, unless you keep time on the edge of your hi-hats.

Some prices
A pair of pro-quality sticks generally cos0ts around seven or eight to fifteen dollars. A professional 14" drum head will set you back about ten to twenty dollars, and most 22" heads sell for around twenty to forty dollars.

SECONDHAND

For a used instrument in mint condition you can expect to pay about half of what it would cost new. Age is not usually the most critical factor in determining the price of secondhand musical instruments. Indeed, sought-after vintage instruments may well sell for similar prices to comparable new ones.

Cymbals
You'll come across plenty of secondhand ride cymbals and hi-hats, whereas crashes and other cymbals are quite rare. Why? Rides and hi-hats hardly ever crack, unlike thinner cymbals such as crashes and splashes. Also, drummers tend to want to replace their rides and hi-hats with cymbals that have different timbres sooner than they replace their crashes.

Privately or from a store?
Used instruments can be found in music stores, but also in pawn shops or advertised in newspapers and music journals, on the Internet, and on bulletin boards in music schools and stores. Purchasing a used instrument from a private individual may be cheaper than buying the same instrument at a store.

Questions
One of the advantages of buying a used instrument in a shop, though, is that you can go back if something turns out not to work properly, or if you have questions. Another difference is that a good dealer will not usually ask an outrageous price, but a private seller might, either because he doesn't know any better, or because he thinks you don't...

WHAT ELSE?

Of course it doesn't hurt to read everything you can find before going out to buy an instrument. But you might end up with just

33

as good an instrument if you simply go into a music store, fall in love with the first set you lay your eyes on, decide that it loves you back as soon as you start playing it, and buy it right away. The instrument you buy should make you feel good. In the end, that counts more than the exact number of plies or the type of wood that has been used. The audience won't notice the technical details of your instrument, but they will know whether or not you're having a good time.

Guideline

Most well-known drummers have one or more endorsements: They play a certain brand of instruments, and the company uses their name for advertising. Such ads can be a good guideline if you're buying stuff. On the other hand, buying the instrument your favorite drummer plays won't make you sound like him or her. It won't even make you play better — unless it makes you feel better.

The music store

A store with an enormous number of instruments on display may be confusing, but a big selection allows for more direct comparisons.

On the other hand, a smaller store may help you focus on the details. So if there are various stores in your area, you may want to visit them all. Listen to a variety of instruments — and listen to a variety of salespeople as well; each has his or her own 'sound' too.

TIP

Another drummer

Whether you're buying new or secondhand, it's a good idea to bring another drummer along. After all, two people see and hear more than one. Having an experienced drummer with you may also reduce the risk of passing up an excellent instrument that needs some repair work — or a lesser-known brand with very strong features. Besides, it's easier to judge the sound of an instrument if you have someone else play it so you can listen from a distance.

Try it out

In a good store you'll be allowed to play-test the instruments. Some stores even have sound-proofed rooms for the purpose. Good stores also have knowledgeable staff who really like their jobs. Good service is important too. For example, can you come back if you have further questions, and will they help you tune the drums they sold you?

Buying online

You can also buy musical instruments online or by mail-order. This makes it impossible to compare instruments, of course, but most online and mail-order companies offer a return service for most or all of their products: If you're not happy with it, you can return it within a certain period of time. Of course the instrument should be in new condition when you send it back.

Catalogs, magazines, Internet

If you want to know all there is to know, then read every instrument review you can find in drummers' and musicians' magazines. Also, stock up with brochures and catalogs. A word of warning, though: Besides having a wealth of information to offer, literature from manufacturers is designed to make you want to spend a lot more than you have, or have in mind — so ask for a price list too. The Internet is a good source for up-to-date product information too. You can find more about these and other resources beginning on page 185.

Fairs and conventions

If a music trade fair or a music convention is being held in your area, check it out. Besides finding a considerable number of instruments that you can try out and compare, you will meet plenty of product specialists, as well as numerous fellow drummers, who are always a source of information and inspiration.

5

Good drums

What a drum sounds like depends on many things, ranging from the shell's material to its diameter, depth and thickness, and to the counter hoops and the lugs. This chapter tells you all there is to look out for when buying a set of drums or a single drum. Hardware follows in Chapter 6, drum heads in Chapter 7, sticks in Chapter 8, and cymbals in Chapter 9.

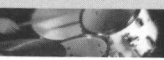

The shell is the basis of any drum. The material, its dimensions, and the way it has been worked can tell you a lot about why a drum sounds the way it does. So that's where this chapter starts, followed by some basic information on different types of lugs and hoops. Specific things to look for in snare drums are on pages 49–52, followed by additional information on bass drums (52–55) and toms and tom mounts (55–61).

Maple and birch

Most bass drums and toms have wooden shells, and so do many snare drums. For professional and medium budget drums, maple is the most popular type of wood, followed by birch. Many pages and hours have been filled with discussions on the differences in sound between these two types of wood — which mainly suggests that those differences aren't really that big.

Blindfold tests

Some drummers say maple sounds warmer, some say birch does. Some find birch more percussive, others will tell you the same about maple. Characteristics such as a wide tuning range have been ascribed to both types of wood as well. Many experts seem to agree that maple makes for a mellower sound and a longer sustain than birch, yet others stress its explosive nature. Likewise, birch drums are sometimes promoted as 'recording drums' — but major recording artists use birch drums on stage too, and even more drummers play maple both live and in the studio. And yes, most drummers fail in blindfold tests when trying to tell whether it's a maple or a birch drum set they're listening to. The moral of this story: Go for the drums and their sound, rather than for a certain type of wood.

Harder and brighter

Other types of wood used include oak (great projection, bright sound), beech (often said to be the happy medium between

birch and maple), mahogany (promotes low-end frequencies), eucalyptus, jatoba, and Australian hardwoods. Generally speaking, the harder the wood is, the brighter and more focused or more articulate the tone of the drum will be.

Maple or maple

Also, note that every type of wood comes in different qualities, and that the quality of the drum has a lot to do with the way the wood is dried, stored, sawn, cut, glued, and finished, too. In other words: You have maple drums, and maple drums…

Not specified

The type of wood on budget drums is usually not specified. As they are made of softer woods (*i.e.*, Filipino mahogany, basswood, or lauan), these drums will usually produce a sound that's often characterized as warm, fat, or round.

Outer and inner plies

Lower mid-range drums may come with one or two plies of maple or birch. An outer ply does more for the looks than for the sound. A hard inner ply can enhance projection, brightness, and definition, and thus improve the sound.

Metal and other materials

Metal shells are used most often for snare drums. Remo is the inventor and sole user of Acousticon, a wood-fiber material of variable hardness, which is used for drum set shells as well as for percussion instruments.

Some companies use other materials, such as carbon fiber, fiberglass or acrylic glass (*e.g.*, Plexiglas). Being hard, these materials generally help produce a louder, brighter sound. They may also make for a greater definition and enhanced durability. Another difference is that some of these drums weigh less than wooden drums.

Shell width

The two main shell dimensions are diameter and depth. The wider a drum is, the lower its tuning range is. Wider drums typically produce a lower pitch.

39

Shell depth

The deeper the shell is, the deeper the drum's sound will be: A 10x12 tom sounds deeper than a tom in the traditional standard size of 8x12. Deeper drums are less responsive: They need more power to speak. Most drum sets come with relatively deep toms (*e.g.*, 10x12) usually known as *power toms*. Other sets feature shallow drums for increased portability.

Thinner and thicker

Most professional drums have relatively thin shells, measuring around $^3/_{16}$" or $^4/_{16}$" (4.5–6.5 mm). It takes good wood and craftsmanship to build shells that thin. That's one of the reasons why most affordable drums have thicker shells, often in the $^5/_{16}$"–$^6/_{16}$" range (8–9.5 mm). Drums with thinner shells tend to speak more easily and produce a warmer, more open, transparent, 'wood' sound. Thicker shells typically promote a more focused or tighter sound with enhanced projection.

Plies

Shells are often made up of six or nine thin plies of wood. For mid and high range shells, the exact number of plies is usually specified.

Drum shells are often made of six or nine plies.

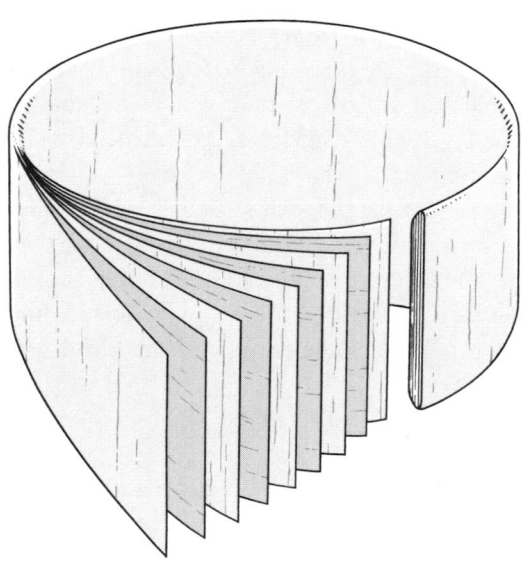

40

Shell thickness and plies

A little theory: Adding extra plies, and so making a shell thicker, stresses the high frequencies in the sound, while you may lose some bottom end. A shell with more plies but the same overall shell thickness will make for a drier, tighter, less responsive or less resonant drum. This is also the result of the extra (non-resonant) adhesive that is required for the additional plies. Conversely, a solid shell, consisting of a single ply only, usually makes for a very responsive drum.

Alternative shell construction

A few smaller companies (Brady, Tamburo, Le Soprano, Troyan, Lignum) use staves to build shells, in a fashion similar to the construction of wooden congas or casks. Usually, but not always, such shells are considerably thicker than plywood shells. Other companies make segment shells, which have wooden segments stacked in way similar to the bricks in a brick wall. Both types of shells tend to be very responsive and resonant.

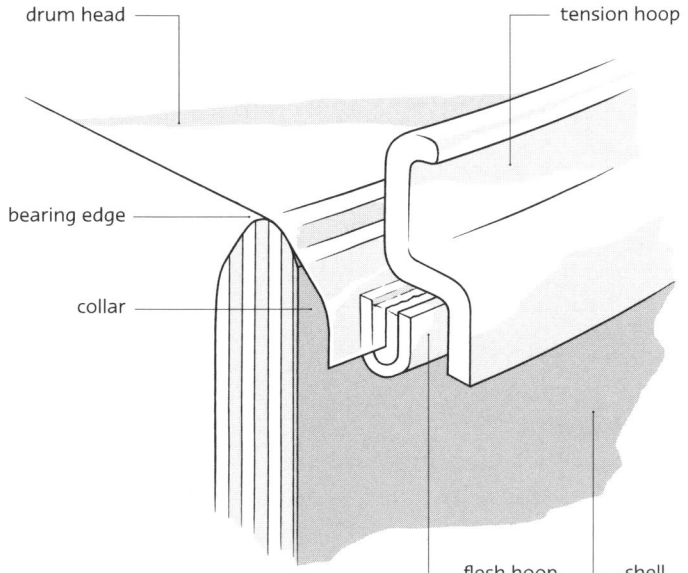

The bearing edge 'bears' the head.

41

The bearing edges

The *bearing edges* of a drum 'bear' the heads. Their exact shape — they are generally angled at 45° — has a noticeable influence on the sound. A sharper edge makes for a 'sharper', brighter sound; rounder edges make for a 'rounder', mellower, less articulate sound. Sharp edges are found on more expensive drums only, not least because it takes longer to make them. No matter what shape they are, bearing edges should always be level and even.

Reinforcement hoops

Some drums have two extra wooden rings on the inside, close to the bearing edges. In the old days they acted as reinforcement rings, keeping the shell from losing its round shape. Nowadays these rings or hoops, with a width of about 1", are largely used to help determine the sound — so they often come with names like *sound rings* or *sound focus rings*. The fact that they increase the shell thickness at the edges is supposed to slightly stress the attack and the higher frequencies.

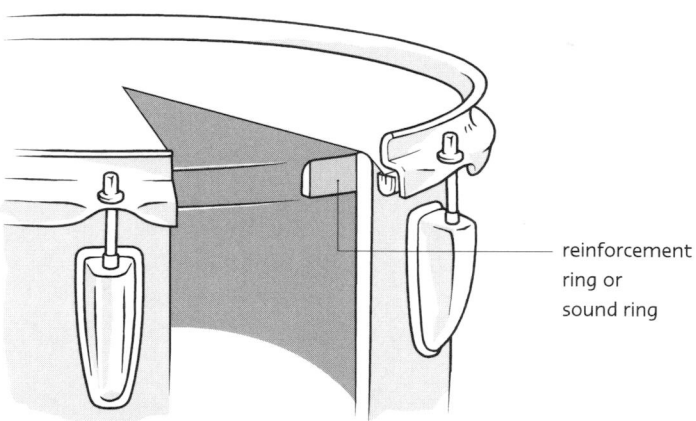

reinforcement ring or sound ring

Custom drums

A few companies offer true custom drums, allowing you to choose shell thickness and shell material per drum, and more. Given this choice, many drummers go for maple bass drums and floor toms, and birch rack toms. Some prefer thicker shells for the

larger drums and thinner shells for their smaller sizes (known as proportionate drums shell thickness); others prefer the opposite, stating that thinner shells on large drums enhances their low-end resonance, while thick shell small toms have more cutting power.

Covered drums

Most lower priced drums come with a plastic wrap finish, which withstands scratches and other damage better than lacquer ever will. Check to see that the covering fits nice and snug all around the shell. The seam should ideally be held under a pair of lugs. This way, the lugs also hide the seam from sight.

Lacquer and wax

Non-covered drums are usually finished with high-gloss solid or transparent lacquers. As an alternative, they may be stained, or — rarely — treated with wax or oil, which gives the shells a matte look. The finish on more expensive drums generally consists of a larger number of coats, which makes it look better and last longer.

> ### Removing the covering
>
> *Covered drums tend to be less responsive than lacquered drums: After all, the covering and the adhesive are non-resonant materials. Removing the warp finish to help the drum sound open up might not be such a good idea: The outer ply of wood this uncovers will not usually be the best surface for a lacquer finish. Lacquered or waxed drums typically have carefully selected outer plies!*

ROUND AND LEVEL

The shell largely determines the quality of sound in a drum by allowing the heads to vibrate as freely as possible. In order to do so, shells should be round and level.

If they're not, the drum may be hard or even impossible to tune.

43

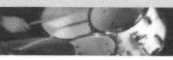
Also, drum shells should be slightly undersized. The following checks are more worthwhile performing on older sets than on new ones.

Undersized? Check

Almost all shells are slightly narrower than the indicated size of the head. This 'floating head design' allows the head to vibrate freely. Simply look at the shell from the side, and see if there's a small, even gap between the shell and the flesh hoop of the head. If there's no such gap, the drum's sound may be restricted. Low-budget covered drums sometimes suffer from this problem.

Bearing edge? Check

Remove the heads and take a close look at the bearing edges, tracing them lightly with a fingertip. If they aren't perfectly even, you may get buzzing sounds when playing the drum. A bit of very careful sanding may help, for instance if the unevenness turns out to be nothing more than a bit of spilled lacquer of glue. Avoid drums with dented edges.

TIPCODE

Tipcode DRUM-003
This Tipcode shows you how to check the bearing edge of a drum.

Round? Check

If the width of the gap between the shell and the flesh hoop of the drum head varies, then either the shell or the flesh hoop isn't as round as it should be. Try replacing the head. Measuring the shell diameter at opposite lugs may show that the drum is not perfectly round — but it's hard to judge this well without some experience and good tools.

44

Tipcode DRUM-004
This Tipcode demonstrates the use of a tape measure to check if a shell isn't out of round.

Level? Check

To see if a shell is level, you need a perfectly level surface. Most tabletops won't do. Take the heads off, put the shell on the surface, insert a light and check to see if there's light shining from under the edge. If you don't trust the flatness of the surface, slowly rotate the drum and see what happens in various positions.

HOOPS AND LUGS

Even the drum's counter hoops and lugs contribute to its sound. Both items come in various designs.

Pressed hoops

The majority of drums come with *pressed counter hoops*, made of steel. Mighty Hoops, Power Hoops and Super Hoops are some of the trade names for pressed hoops that are slightly heavier (usually around ³⁄₁₆" or 2.3 mm thick). They may add a bit to the attack and make the sound a bit 'heavier' and drier. Also, their increased thickness helps prevent warping.

Die-cast hoops

Die-cast hoops don't warp at all. You mainly find these very heavy hoops on more expensive snare drums, which is where they're considered to be most effective, adding extra solidity, weight and definition to rim shots and stick shots.

45

Some companies have die-cast hoops on their toms too, often in more expensive series only.

Die-cast hoop (left) and pressed hoops look very different.

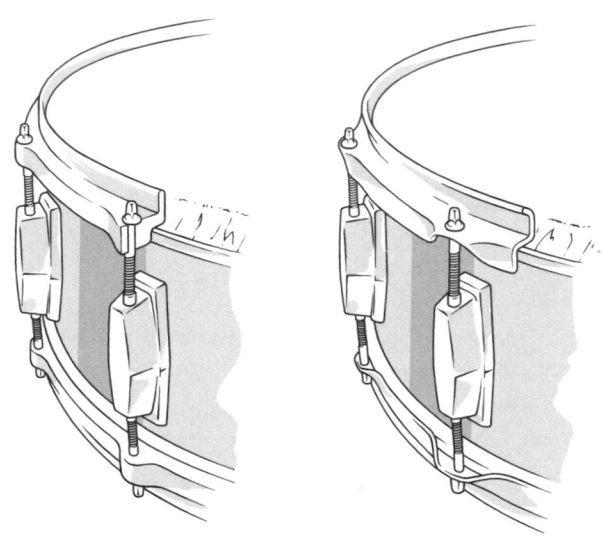

Triple-flanged hoops

Pressed hoops usually have three flanges: They're known as triple-flanged hoops. The upper one, which protects your sticks from the biting effect of rim shots, was added last: Historically speaking, this is the third flange.

Triple-flanged hoop

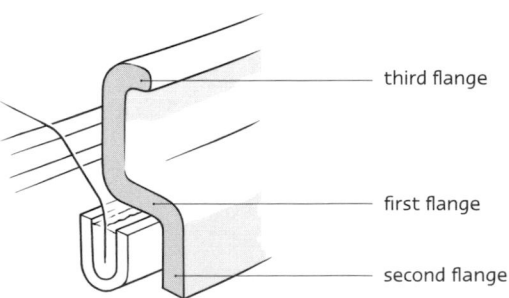

Wooden hoops

Most bass drums have wooden hoops. Less expensive ones often come with synthetic or metal hoops (see page 54). Wooden hoops

can be found on some expensive snare drums too, and there are a few sets available that even have wooden hoops on the toms. On these drums, wooden hoops help produce a very warm, 'woody' sound.

Single lugs
Drums can often be recognized by their lugs, which come in all kinds of shapes and sizes. Most new drums have relatively small lugs, known as *single lugs*; there's one row of single lugs for each head, each lug receiving a single tension bolt.

Double lugs
Up until the mid-1990s, many drums had *long lugs* or *double lugs*, which receive a tension bolt at either end. These lugs are also known as *flush bracing* or *high-tension lugs* — even though the very moderate tension on the average drum head does not really justify the term 'high tension'.

Drums with tube lugs, small lugs, and long lugs.

Fashion and taste
The choice between single and double lugs depends on fashion and taste more than anything else, and the same goes for variations such as the tiny *low-mass lug* or the 'classic' *tube lug*, the latter being no more than a tube with threaded ends. Some companies make all their series, from entry-level to top of the line, look similar by using the same type of lug on all of the drums; other companies do the opposite, giving every series they make a unique look.

47

Self-aligning nuts

The *self-aligning nuts* in most lugs help prevent you from damaging the thread of both nuts and tension rods, and they also adjust to slightly different hoop sizes. These nuts are kept in place by plastic inserts, which often double as anti-detune devices by exerting slight pressure on the tension rods.

Lugs often have plastic inserts.

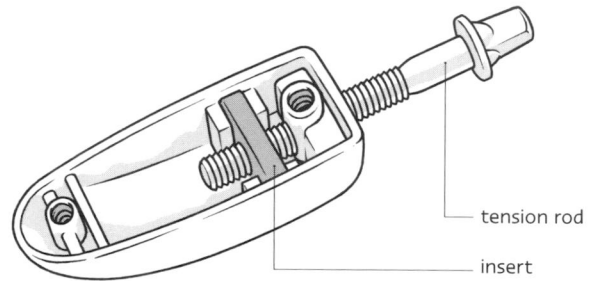

tension rod

insert

How many?

Most 22" bass drums and 14" snares have ten lugs for each head. Toms up to 13" usually have six, and larger toms come with eight. Cheaper drums may have fewer lugs, which doesn't affect the ease of tuning or the tuning stability as much as you might think.

A coarser sound

Some high-end snare drums have eight lugs per head too, rather than ten — not to cut costs but to produce a sound that may be described as coarser or more open. Some brands use five lugs on their (professional) 10" toms. This doesn't harm the sound or the tuning stability, but it may take some getting used to when tuning.

Gaskets

Small rubber or plastic gaskets underneath the lugs are sometimes promoted as sound enhancing items, but their main task is to prevent the lugs from damaging the finish or the wooden shell. Most wrap finish drums come without such gaskets.

Plating and coating

Traditionally, all hardware is chrome plated. Chrome is typically more durable and less susceptible to scratching than most other

48

finishes, including black chrome. Gold plating is softer than chrome plating. Solid brass is what it is: solid brass.

Triple chrome plating

High quality chrome will last for many, many years, but it's hard to tell good chrome. What you can see is whether a lot of polishing has been done: If so, the surface looks like a mirror, rather than like rippled water. The term triple chrome plating *is often used in ads — but basically, chrome plating always involves three steps: plating the metal with one or two layers of nickel (or nickel and copper) to resist corrosion, followed by the actual chrome plating.*

THE SNARE DRUM

The snare drum is the most personal drum of your set; that's why professional touring drummers who don't bring their own sets will still often take their own snare drums (next to their cymbals and bass drum pedal!). It also explains why many drummers have more than one snare drum, so they can pick a specific sound for a specific style, mood, or sound — a shallow one with a tight sound for funky stuff, a deep one for major backbeats.

Replace

In entry-level sets, the snare is most often the one drum that doesn't match the quality of the rest of the set. Drummers often replace it with a better one as soon as their budget permits. But listen carefully to the original drum first: Make sure it gets a professional quality batter head and tune it, or have it tuned properly. Some cheap snare drums sound much better than their price would make you think.

Material

Snare drums come in a dazzling variety of shell materials, sizes

49

and configurations. Compared to wood, metal shells sound brighter and project better. Most metal snares have steel shells. Brass and bronze are generally said to make for a slightly mellower sound. Wood shell snare drums tend to sound warmer, fatter, and 'woodier'.

Shell depth

The best-selling snare drum sizes are between 5x14 and 6.5x14. The deeper the shell, the deeper the sound. For a really meaty, beefy sound you could try a 8x14, though drums this size are quite rare. A deeper shell doesn't allow you to play louder — but a shallow snare drum is typically more responsive, allowing you to play softer...

Smaller snare drums

Smaller, high-pitched snares are mainly used as add-ons, often positioned to the left of the hi-hat. *Piccolos* are most popular for that purpose, ranging in size from 3x13 up to 4x14. Even smaller snare drums, with 12" or 10" heads, come with non-standardized names like *soprano* and *sopranino*. Again, depth is a major factor. A 7x12 drum, for example, will produce a rather deep, yet high-pitched sound.

8x14 and 3.5x14 snare drums.

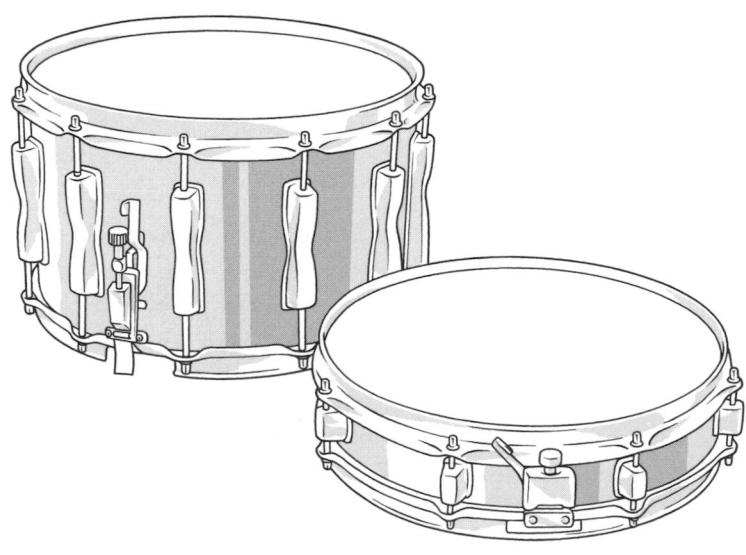

50

Snare strainer

Most snare strainers are quite straightforward *throw-off* affairs, and that's basically all you need. They shouldn't rattle in the 'off' position, and they're supposed to operate quietly and easily, without any need to hold the drum with your other hand to keep it from falling over when switching the snares on or off.

Tension

Good strainers allow you to adjust snare tension with the snares 'on'. If so, adjust the tension while tapping the head. This allows you to hear exactly what you're doing. Tension knobs on both the strainer and the *butt end* (which holds the snares on the other side of the drum) make it easier to center the snares. There's more on this in Chapter 10, *Tuning and muffling*.

Strings or straps

The snappy snares can be attached with either strings or straps. Strings are more likely to break, but both strings and straps usually last for years. Some strainers/butt ends accept both strings and straps. Experiment, and you may find that straps produce a tighter snare response, for example. *Tip:* some strainers allow you to remove the snares without any tools, which makes snare head changes easier.

Centered

When trying out snare drums, always check that the snares are centered, with either end at an equal distance from the edge. To find out whether the tension on the snares is the same left and right, gently compare the tension on the outer snares. Really gently: If you accidentally overstretch a strand, it will rattle as you play; removing it will be your only option.

Snare bed

For a non-buzzing, tight and crisp sound, the snares should touch the bottom head over their entire length. Snare drum shells have been modeled for this purpose: They're a bit shallower where the strings or straps run over the drum's edge (see next page!). Because of this so-called snare bed the snare-side head surface is slightly concave, allowing for optimal head-to-snare contact.

51

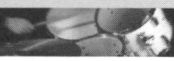

The snare bed:
the shell is a
little shallower
where the
strings run over
the edges.

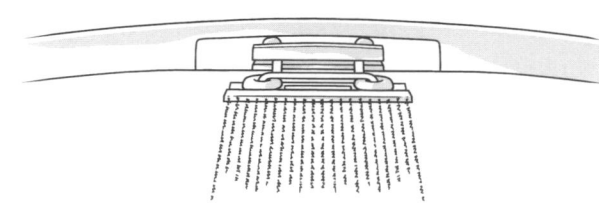

> ## Parallel action
>
> Parallel action strainers *are quite complicated snare systems
> that keep the snares under tension while in the 'off' position.
> The snares extend over the edges of the drum (as if you're
> using 15" snares on a 14" drum), which is typically said to
> promote the response of the instrument. Parallel action
> strainers have been very popular for some years, but they've
> become rare. The same goes for the so-called* semi-parallel
> *strainers, which combined extended snares and a less
> complicated mechanism.*

THE BASS DRUM

The bigger the drum, the lower it will sound. And the longer. For
bass drums low is okay, but long isn't. That's why most drummers
muffle their bass drums, making for a rather short, though big,
punchy, and solid sound.

Sizing it up

Bass drums have become deeper over time. For many years, 14x22
was the best-selling size. Then came the 16x22, followed by the
18x22. The idea is to create a bass drum with plenty of bottom end
without losing focus or definition. Traditionally, jazz drummers go
for small bass drums (14x18 or 16x18) with a rather high tuning.

In between, or bigger

The 20" bass drum, producing more low end than an 18" and

52

more focus than a 22", gained popularity when fusion took off. If you like lots of low end you may want to try a 24" or even the occasional 26".

Deeper

Bass drum shell depths usually vary from 14" (still known as standard depth) to 18" or more, the extra inches mainly adding to the depth of the sound.

Sub-woofer

For an even punchier, low-end sound, DW pioneered the Woofer, an 8" bass drum with a built-in microphone. The drum is positioned in front of the regular bass drum.

Kits for kids

A kit with an 18" or even a 16" bass drum can be a great 'junior' drum set. In the lower price ranges, however, 18" bass drums are hard to find. There are special drum sets for kids too, but they're often of a lesser quality than the average entry-level instrument. If kids are serious about drumming, buy them a 'serious' junior instrument, rather than a toy drum set!

Tension rods

In the past, bass drums were always tuned using T-rods. By the late 1990s most of these had been replaced by standard key rods, which

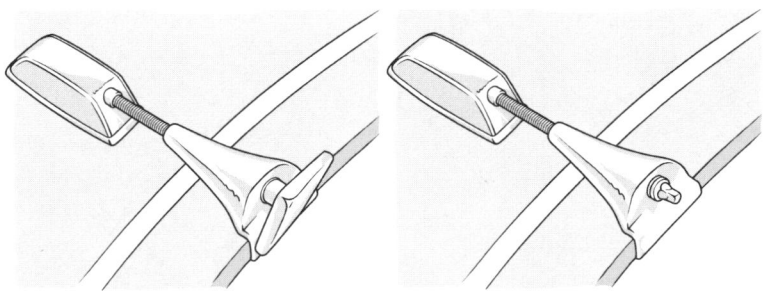

A traditional T-rod and a standard key rod on a bass drum hoop.

53

take up less space on the road and give the drum a cleaner look: It is impossible to fine-tune your bass drum heads while keeping all T-handles in line with the bass drum hoop.

Fast adjustment

On the other hand, T-rods do allow for fast adjustment of the bass drum tuning *and* sound — which you may want to do quite often, as bass drums tend to be more dependent on room acoustics than any of your other drums. Also, often just a few turns on one or two T-rods on the batter side are all you need to give a bass drum a fat, dry sound for some songs or a higher, more resonant tone for others.

Hoops

Most entry-level sets come with hollow metal bass drum hoops, with a small rubber insert to allow proper attachment of the bass drum pedal. Wooden hoops, as found in higher price ranges, add a bit of warmth to the sound of the drum. In between are hoops made of synthetic materials such as ABS. They may not look as good as wood, but they're not as vulnerable and they don't make for a different sound, really.

Claw hooks

Wooden hoops are easily damaged, if not by bumping things against them, then by the *claw hooks*, which rarely fit the profile of the hoop like a glove. A tip? When replacing bass drum heads, always put the hoops back in their original position, so the claws don't make unnecessary marks on the hoop. Some high-end sets feature die-cast claws hooks, instead of standard pressed ones, and

A wooden hoop with claw hooks and a plastic one with 'ears'.

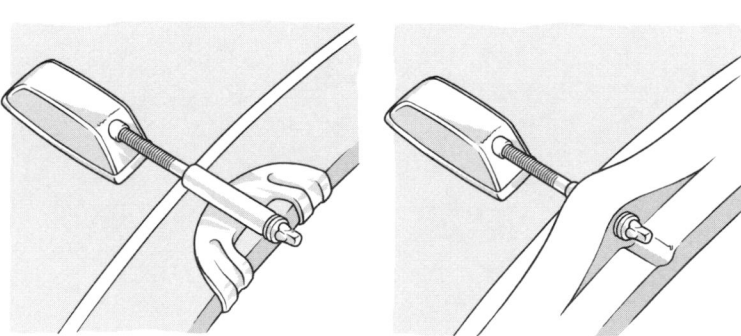

an occasional set comes with felt inlays in the hooks. Plastic hoops don't use claw hooks at all; they have 'built-in' ears, just like tom and snare drum hoops.

Spurs

Though some spurs may look very impressive, they don't do much more than prevent the bass drum from rolling over or sliding away from you. Most designs offer one preset angle, which is basically all you need. Setting the height of the spurs is something you usually do just once, eliminating the need for all kinds of memory features.

Convertible design

Bass drums spurs have a convertible design, allowing you to use sharp metal spikes (with care — on wooden floors or carpets) or rubber feet (on other surfaces — and when moving your drums!). Usually this is a matter of screwing the rubber feet up or down along the threaded end of the spurs. Bayonet catches are easier, but they're rare. Some floor tom legs come with convertible feet too. As there is no forward motion to stop, these spike tips seem to make less sense than the ones on bass drum spurs.

Toms on the bass drum?

On some higher end sets, the rack toms are to be mounted on separate stands or on a *drum rack*, rather than on the bass drum. Why? Because the bass drum sound is believed to be enhanced by relieving it of the strain of one or two toms resting on it — which is open to discussion as long as the bass drum is as muffled as it usually is. More importantly, many high-end bass drums have very thin shells that are not designed to carry the weight of two toms plus a holder. There's more about drum racks on page 81.

TOMS

Rack toms and floor toms are available in an incredibly wide variety of sizes, some series even featuring a choice of three or more shell depths for each diameter.

Tom sizes

The most extended drum series offer toms from 8" up to 16" or even 18". The only uneven sizes are 13" and 15". Occasionally, 6" toms are available too. Tama made an 11" tom for a while.

12" and 13"

The 'standard' drum set, as it has been sold for many years, comes with 12" and 13" rack toms, which are quite close in size, and therefore in pitch. The 16" floor tom that comes with this standard setup is substantially bigger, and lower. As a result, the pitch difference between the two rack toms will be much smaller than the pitch difference between the 13" and the 16". Want to know more? Check out Chapter 10, *Tuning and muffling.*

Fusion and other sizes

As an alternative, you may go for what's typically known as a fusion set. These setups have smaller toms, usually with head sizes two inches apart, *e.g.,* 10" and 12" rack toms, and a 14" (floor) toms.

Smaller, not higher

In most series — except for budget series — you can pick your own combination of shell sizes. Do note that pitch is not the only consideration. An example. In a traditional jazz setup, the first tom (12"), will usually be tuned considerably higher than rock drummers tend to tune their (smaller!) 10" tom. The higher tuning not only makes for a higher pitch, but for a very different timbre as well — even if both drums are from the same brand and series. A 12" with a relatively high tuning will produce a bright, tight sound with lots of attack, while a low tuned 10" sounds warm and kind of fat, and often 'bigger' than it really is.

Shell depths

Drums come in different shell depths. Many semi-pro and pro series offer you a choice of two depths for each shell size; some high-end series have even more options. Taking a 12" tom as an example, here's what you may come across:

- The traditional **standard size**, 8x12, is mainly used in jazz and fusion.

- The description **power toms** generally refers to two variations, 11x12 and, more commonly, 10x12; these have been the most popular sizes for years.

- An in-between size, 9x12, started to gain popularity in the late 1990s, usually marketed under names that suggest a **fast response**. (A traditional 8x12, however, will always be even faster). Sets featuring these in-between sizes usually have shallow floor toms (*e.g.*, 13x16).

- The deepest toms have **symmetrical** or **square** sizes (12x12).

- Then there are drum sets designed for easy transportation, a tight sound, or both, featuring **very shallow** drums (including a 5x12 tom, for example).

- … and there are also drums that have **no shells at all**, each drum consisting of nothing but a round frame, a tuning system and a head.

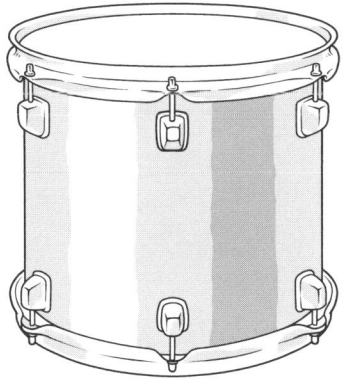 

Toms come in a variety of depths: a 10x12 power tom and a standard size, 8x12.

Floor toms

The most popular floor tom is the 16x16, followed by the 14x14. Much less common are 18" and 15" toms, but some companies make these sizes too. Floor toms usually have square sizes, but there are shallow models as well (promoting a faster response; see above). Extra deep floor toms (17x15, 16x14) have also been produced. Most 18" floor toms are 16" deep. An 18x18 would hardly leave any room between the bottom head and the floor, preventing

the sound from developing. The response of a drum that size would be rather sluggish, too.

> ### Suspended floor toms
>
> *In the late 1980s and early 1990s, many drummers, especially in fusion, replaced their floor toms by slightly shallower drums that were mounted on a stand, increasing the response as well as floor space. The 12x14 and 13x15 are the most popular sizes in these type of drums, commonly known as hanging or suspended floor toms.*

TOM HOLDERS

Most drummers mount their rack toms on the bass drum, rather than using separate stands or a drum rack. Many of today's tom holders or *tom mounts* incorporate some kind of isolated mounting system, which prevents the hardware from absorbing most of the sound of the toms.

Tubes and rods

Loads of entry-level sets come with tom holders modeled on a very

Different tom holders: one with an L-rod (left), and a Pearl design (right), the latter with a disengaged memory lock.

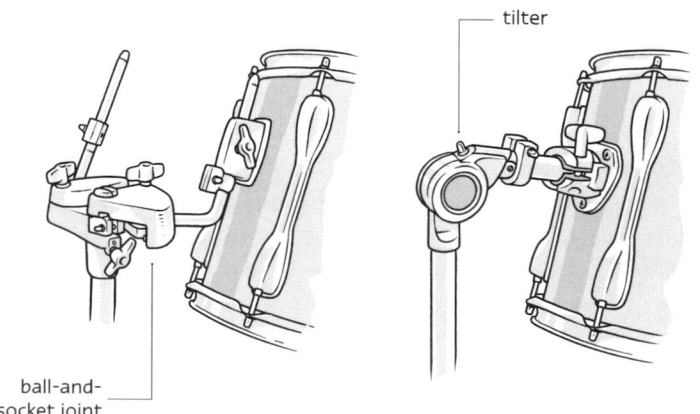

tilter

ball-and-socket joint

basic yet effective Pearl design, which consists basically of two sets of two tubes, each with a tilter in the middle. Another basic design involves one center post and two L-shaped rods for the toms. Contrary to the aforementioned design, these L-rods do not intrude the shells. Most other holders are a combination of these two systems.

Toothless tilters

The tilters are most often *ratchet tilters*, which use two sets of interlocking 'teeth'. *Toothless tilters* offer finer and faster adjustment. *Ball-and-socket joints* do so too. One advantage of ball-and-socket joints is that they allow for omni-directional adjustment using just one thumbscrew. Apart from the ease of adjustment, the actual differences between tom holders aren't that big, and bad ones are hard to find.

Tipcode DRUM-005
This Tipcode shows you the flexibility of a ball-and-socket joint.

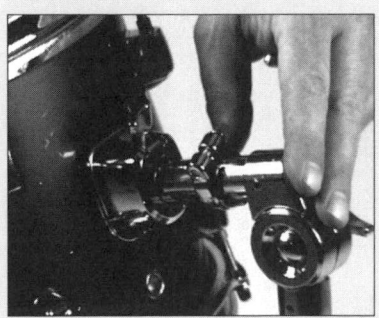

Tipcode DRUM-006
Play this Tipcode to see how to set and use a memory lock (see the next page).

59

Memory locks

Tom holders always come with small metal clamps that 'memorize' your settings, allowing you to set up fast, while also adding to the stability. Some of the original trade names (*e.g.*, *memory locks*, *key locks*, or *stop locks*) have become generic names. Memory locks are also used on hi-hat pedals, for example.

Memory lock on a tom holder.

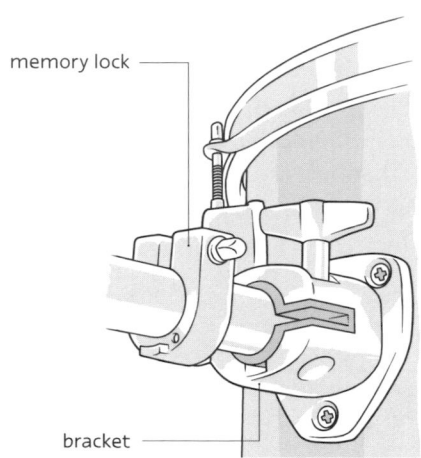

memory lock

bracket

Disappearing vibrations

If the tom bracket is attached directly to the shell, you may experience a notable loss of tone and sustain when you mount the drum on its holder. The test: Tune a small tom, play it and listen to its sound while holding it by the hoop. Then mount it on the tom holder and listen again. If you hear a difference — and you will — the reason is that it's not only the heads that vibrate, the shell does too. If the bracket is attached directly to the shell of the drum, a lot of these vibrations will be absorbed by the mass of the metal of the bracket and the tom holder.

Isolated tom mounting

In the early 1980s drummer Gary Gauger introduced a solution to this problem. In his Resonance Isolation Mounting System (RIMS), the toms are mounted in rubber, hanging from their tension rods. The original tom bracket is attached to a side plate. This acoustical suspension or resonance isolating tom mounting allows a drum to produce the fullest sound possible.

Tom
mounted in
RIMS.

Other systems

Many drum companies have come up with their own solutions, collectively known as *isolated mounting systems*. Others use (copies of) the original RIMS. *Tip:* Isolated mounting systems also help reduce cross talk, meaning that hitting one drum will be less likely to make one or more of the other drums sound along. This is especially important when close miking the drum set.

Floor toms

Though floor toms may also benefit from isolated mounting, the effect on rack toms is much larger. Some brands do offer special floor tom legs to allow greater resonance from these drums.

LISTEN UP

Once you know what you're looking for, it's time to start listening to the drums. Here are some tips.

The same heads

When comparing drums, use the same or similar heads on them. If not, you're comparing heads more than you are comparing

61

drums: After all, the heads account for most of the sound of the drum. Also make sure the drums have similar tunings. In Chapter 10 you'll find that this involves more than tuning them to roughly the same pitch.

> ## The best heads
>
> *If you want to hear what the drums really sound like, it's best to use medium clear heads on the toms and a medium coated head on the snare drum, both without any muffling: Muffling makes drums sound nice and fat, but also very much alike. Please refer to Chapter 7 for examples of the various types of heads.*

Isolated mounting

If you compare a drum set with an isolated mounting system to one without this feature, the latter is likely to lose out, even if it's a much more expensive set — but then you're comparing mounting systems rather than drums.

The difference

What does money buy you, in terms of sound? Higher-priced sets offer what's often referred to as a richer sound. There are lots of lows, mids, and highs in the sound, and they're all in balance. This is what makes the instrument speak, as it's sometimes described, and what turns it into a really musical instrument. On a good drum set you will hear each note on each particular drum, even in the fastest rolls you can play, without things getting muddy. Drums that speak well also project well; their sound will cut through, and you're less likely to need amplification when playing in a band.

Timbre

The exact mix between lows, mids and highs determines the instrument's timbre, or the 'color' of its voice — whether it sounds fat, dark, green, bright, transparent, solid, sweet, subdued, yellow,

62

or harsh. This is where it comes to taste, really. There's no such thing as a typical rock drum, a typical jazz drum, a typical studio drum, or whatever. What makes a 'typical' fusion drum set or a 'typical' heavy metal drum set are the sizes, the heads and the tuning — not the drums themselves.

Sustain, attack, response

When testing drums, play them as loudly and as softly as you plan to play them. Listen to the balance between the attack (the initial sound of the stick hitting the head) and the tone (which is what follows). Also listen to how easily the drums respond. If you do quiet gigs too, drums should be able to sound at their fullest even when played softly.

Tuning

Tune the drums the way you plan to play them. If you've got a sensitive ear you can compare tuning ranges as well. How high and how low do the drums go, without losing their tone? Contrary to popular belief, you may find that expensive drums are not easier to tune than budget instruments. It's the other way around, actually; it takes more time (and tuning experience) to balance out the wider range of frequencies that high-end drums are capable of producing.

Everything

What a drum sounds like is determined by everything that is attached to it, and by the way it has been made. The number of plies, the shell thickness, the bearing edge, the type of wood, the finish, the hoops, the heads, the lugs… So in the end, after having discussed, researched, and enjoyed all its details, you simply need to listen to the instrument as a whole — because that's what you'll end up playing.

Too long

After playing various drum sets for fifteen minutes or half an hour, you'll hardly be able to really listen to all the subtle differences between one instrument and the other anymore. Take a break, or come back the next day. Also, try not to compare too many instruments at a time. Instead, select three snare drums,

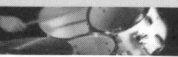

for example; play them for a while; replace the one you like least — and so on.

SECONDHAND

Pretty much everything that has been said above also goes for used drums and drum sets. Of course there are a few special things to pay attention to when buying a pre-owned instrument.

- Check if everything is **complete and in working order**. Are all the hoops, lugs and tension rods present? A used bass drum may have lost its front head and everything that's supposed to come with it.

- Check if the drums **tune properly and easily**. If not, check the heads. Also, the shell and the hoops should be perfectly round and level. Do check the bearing edges too.

- The condition of the **finish** often indicates how carefully the set has been treated. Check wooden hoops, especially, and see if the snare drum hasn't scratched the lacquer from the left-side rack tom.

- Drum sets can live to a **ripe old age**. Twenty or thirty years or more is no problem, provided they have been treated with care. Expanding used sets with matching drums may be a problem however, especially — but not only — in the lower price ranges.

- The **brand name on the heads** says nothing about the brand of the drums!

- Older used sets may come with **single-headed toms**, also known as *concert toms* or *melodic toms*. These have a short, not very resonant sound.

- The lug nuts of older sets may be kept in place by **springs**, rather than by nylon inserts (see page 48). These springs tend to vibrate along with each beat, unless they have been muffled with plastic tubing or small pieces of foam plastic.

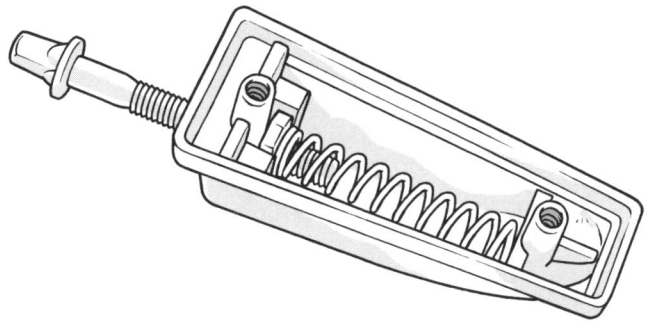

• European drums from the 1960s or earlier may have **metric sizes**. Fitting drum heads can be made to order, but they're expensive.

6

Hardware

The key requirements for stands, pedals, and all other hardware items are pretty basic: Every piece of hardware should be stable, sturdy, easily adjustable, and noiseless.

If a drum set comes with hardware, check out all the separate items. Some cheaper drum sets come with nice stands but have awkward pedals, for instance, while others offer less quantity (the stands are not as heavy) but more quality (everything works better and pedals move faster). Another tip: If you're not an extremely heavy hitter, you probably won't need extremely heavy, bulky stands.

Hardware sets

If hardware is not included, most brands offer two or three hardware sets which you can choose from, but of course you're free to go for another brand too. However, using accessories and instruments from one brand only may improve the looks of your set, as everything is likely to have the same styling. The tom holder usually comes with the drums, so this piece of hardware has been dealt with in Chapter 5.

BASS DRUM PEDALS

A snare drum is your most personal drum, your ride cymbal your most personal cymbal, and your bass drum pedal is your most personal piece of hardware.
Good mid-range pedals that can take you through any gig are available for some hundred to hundred twenty-five dollars, but you can also spend much more.

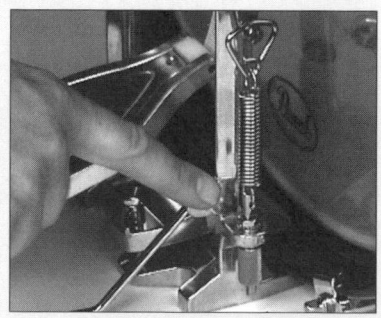

Tipcode DRUM-007
This is how to adjust and lock the spring tension of a bass drum pedal.

68

Spring tension

Every bass drum pedal comes with an adjustable spring. The higher the tension, the harder you'll have to work to depress the pedal, and the quicker the beater will return. Usually, drummers with a 'heavier foot' use higher spring tensions, and vice versa. As always, there are numerous exceptions to this rule.

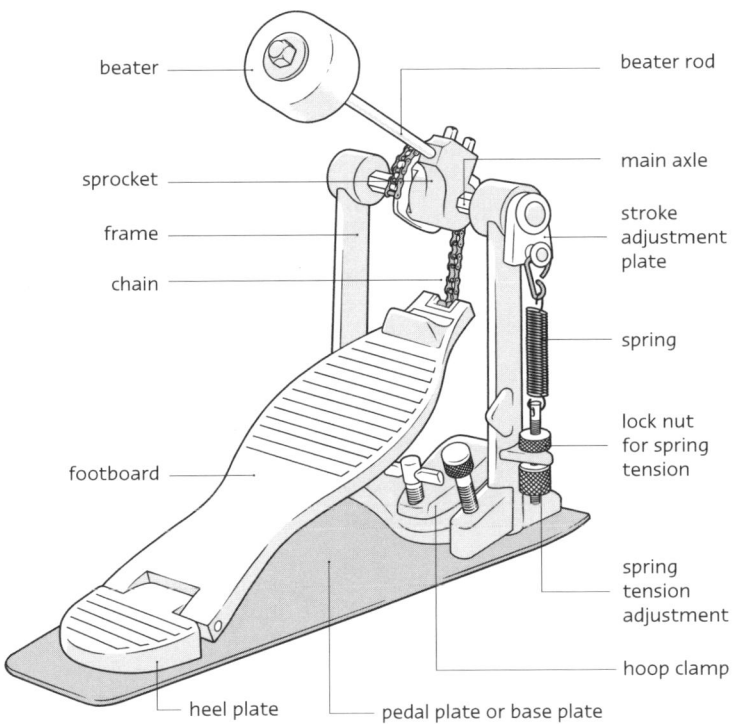

Bass drum pedal.

beater — beater rod
sprocket — main axle
frame — stroke adjustment plate
chain — spring
footboard — lock nut for spring tension
— spring tension adjustment
heel plate — hoop clamp
pedal plate or base plate

A bass drum pedal with a regular chain drive system (L), and one with an eccentric sprocket. Note the different beaters.

Chain or strap

Pedals basically come in two versions: They're either chain-driven, or they employ a fabric drive strap to drive the beater towards your bass drum head. These types feel different, and not just because the material is different: The entire assembly is different, too.

Chain

On most *chain-driven pedals*, the chain runs over a round sprocket or over a round cam, with the main axle passing through the sprocket's center. This makes for a very even feel or action.

69

Strap

Strap-driven pedals, on the other hand, often have what's known as an *eccentric cam.* This results in a lighter action, the footboard traveling a little further. There are also chain-driven pedals with eccentric sprockets, usually providing an action somewhere between the other two types.

A bass drum pedal with a regular chain drive system (L), and one with an eccentric cam. Note the different beaters.

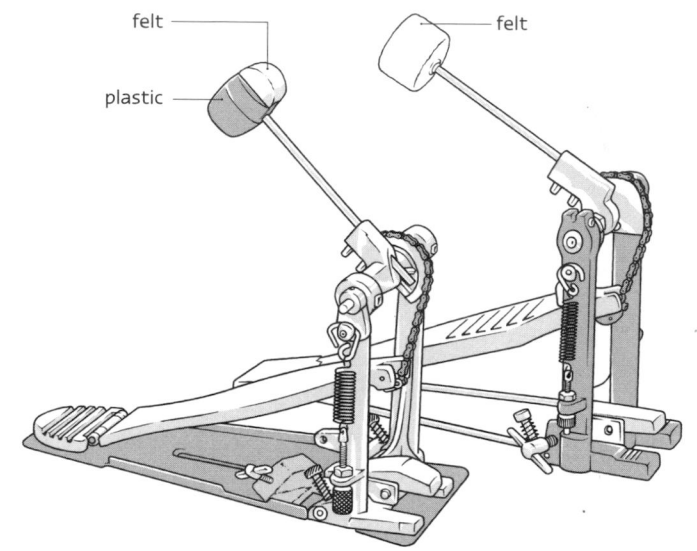

felt

felt

plastic

Which one?

A 'heavy' drummer may use a pedal with a relatively light action,

TIP

Adjustable action

Very few pedals feature an adjustable action, which influences not only the feel of the pedal, but the resulting sound as well. Adjusting it to a heavier feel will usually help produce a heavier sound too, depending on the construction of the pedal and the range of adjustment. Playing around with the settings of such pedals may help you find out whether you like a heavier or a lighter action — and once you decide what you prefer, you may realize you don't need a pedal with an adjustable action at all.

70

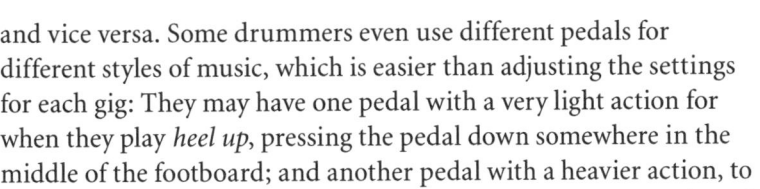

and vice versa. Some drummers even use different pedals for different styles of music, which is easier than adjusting the settings for each gig: They may have one pedal with a very light action for when they play *heel up*, pressing the pedal down somewhere in the middle of the footboard; and another pedal with a heavier action, to be used when they play *heel down*, their entire foot on the footboard, using all the leverage the pedal provides — or vice versa...

Lighter action, lighter spring setting?

If a pedal 'feels' too heavy, can't you just lower the spring tension? Yes and no. Yes, because that will make for a lighter feel. And no, because the spring tension also influences the way the beater comes back to you — unlike adjusting the action, for example. Conversely, adjusting the action usually influences the distance your footboard has to travel. Adjusting the spring tension does not.

Chains and teeth

The sprocket wheel that chain-driven pedals traditionally used to come with, has gradually been replaced by less noisy, felt-lined wheels (i.e., *chain channel*), either with or without a couple of 'guiding' teeth. If there are any teeth, check that the chain matches them. As chains are unlikely to break, life expectancy isn't necessarily using a very heavy chain, or a double chain. Double chains, however, may add stability to the pedal action.

Stability

The more stable a pedal is, the more efficiently your energy will be translated into sound. A *base plate* (also known as *pedal plate* or *stabilizer plate*) will help, and it also helps reducing unwanted noise. Pedals with base plates take up more room in transportation, and they're a bit hard to attach to the bass drum if the thumbscrew is located in its traditional place, under the footboard. On an increasing number of pedals the thumbscrew has been moved to the side (see the illustrations on page 72), making it easier to attach the pedal to the hoop.

Prime adjustments

The beater is usually set at its maximum height, or just a little lower. On bass drum pedals, spring tension is always adjustable.

A pedal with a base plate, the thumbscrew mounted to the side of the footboard (left), and one without a base plate, with the thumbscrew under the footboard (right).

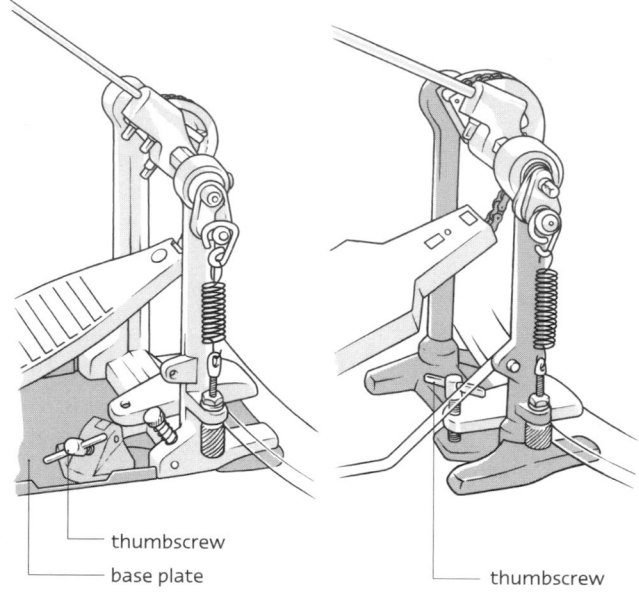

thumbscrew

base plate

thumbscrew

When comparing pedals, set the springs to identical tensions. Only a few pedals offer some type of interlocking adjustment screw that really secures the spring tension setting.

Beater and footboard angle

The larger the beater angle, the longer the stroke of the beater will be, and the louder you can play. Many pedals offer three or four beater angle positions, corresponding to the number of holes in the *stroke adjustment plate* or *spring swivel*. If there's a slot instead of a couple of holes, you can make finer adjustments. When changing this setting, the footboard angle often changes too: If you increase the stroke, the front of the footboard will come up — which may not be what you want. Unfortunately, there are only a few pedals on which both angles can be set independently.

The beater

The beater itself is important for the sound and the feel of the pedal. The harder it is, the clearer or brighter the attack will be, and the more need there is for a protective pad on the bass drum head. Beaters come in felt, plastic, and wood, and some have interchangeable beater surfaces. Felt beaters, the most popular

72

choice, come in different hardnesses. Cheaper beaters are usually quite soft, producing a mushier sound with less attack. They wear down faster too. Beaters also differ in weight. A heavier beater feels different from a lighter one: It promotes the impact but slows down the action of the pedal. There are special weights available that attach to the beater rod. The higher up you attach the weight, the heavier the beater impact will be.

Bearings
A good pedal only moves where it's supposed to move, in the direction it's supposed to move in. Unwanted play or give in the moving parts will absorb at least some of your energy. More importantly, any type of play is bound to get worse. The use of bearings, for instance in the heel joint, prevents play from developing.

Smooth
The action of a bass drum pedal is meant to be smooth and noiseless. The ultimate test? Put it on the counter and move the footboard up and down with your hand. That way you'll hear any noises that shouldn't be there, and you'll easily feel even the slightest irregularities in the pedal's action.

Spurs, spikes, or Velcro
To keep them from moving forward, pedals usually have either retractable *spurs* or *spikes*, or a coarse type of Velcro (known as industrial Velcro) or rubber underneath the base plate.

Double pedal.

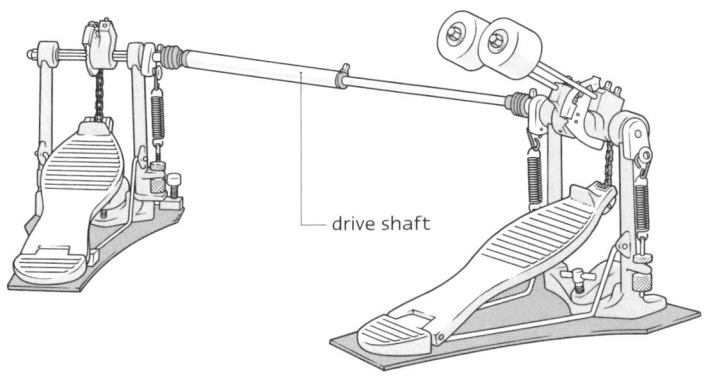

drive shaft

73

Double pedals

So-called *double bass drum pedals* allow you to use both feet to play the bass drum. When selecting such a pedal, always feel for play in and around the shaft that connects both pedals. Hold the cam or the sprocket of the auxiliary pedal, and try to move the auxiliary beater. If there's any play, it's bound to get worse. Very few pedals come with ball bearings in the U-joints of the shaft that connects the pedals. Without such bearings, the drive shaft won't last for years.

HI-HAT PEDALS

You should judge a hi-hat pedal in much the same way as you would a bass drum pedal. The number of adjustments is usually much smaller, however.

Spring tension

Some budget hi-hat pedals come with non-adjustable springs. If the spring tension is too light for the cymbals you're using, the action will be slow. If it's too heavy, you'll have to work too hard. In other words, you're usually better off getting an adjustable one, for which you'll likely pay seventy-five to a hundred dollars or more.

The tilter

When closing your hi-hats cymbals, you may hear 'zomp' rather

TIPCODE

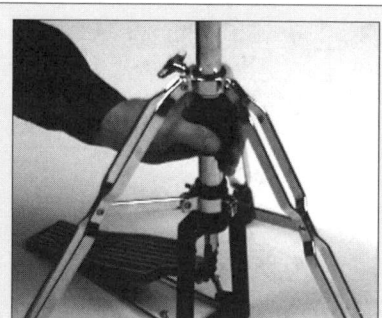

Tipcode DRUM-008
A hi-hat pedal with adjustable spring tension is shown in this Tipcode.

than the commonly desired 'chick' sound. Usually, this is the result of what's known as *air-lock*, the air between the cymbals acting as a cushion between the two cymbals. To prevent this, the bottom cymbal can be tilted. Most tilters use a set screw that slightly tilts a metal washer under the bottom cymbal. *Tip:* There are also hi-hat cymbals that have been designed to prevent air-lock (see Chapter 9).

A tilter for the bottom cymbal.

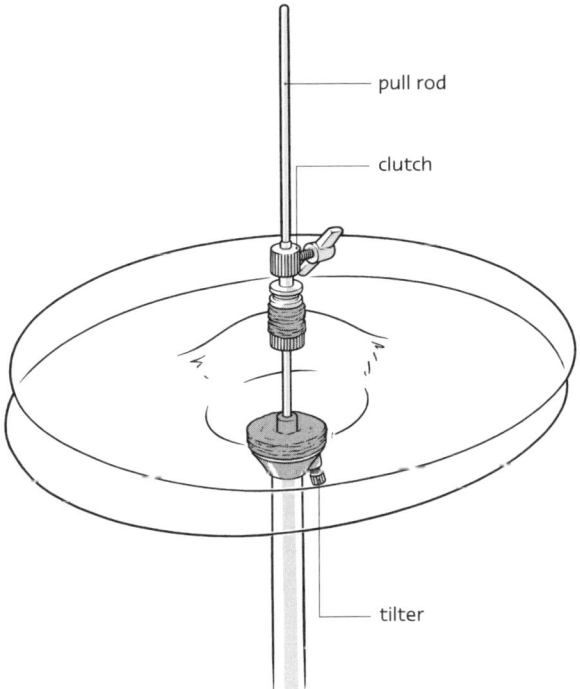

pull rod

clutch

tilter

Clutches

The top cymbal is attached to the *pull rod* with a *clutch*. Even the most basic clutches will do in most cases. Some are more expensive because of their looks; others feature a special type of bolt to give them extra grip on the pull rod, or a system preventing the nuts (and eventually the top cymbal) from coming loose.

Felts

The harder the felts that hold the top cymbal, the brighter the sound will be. The same goes for the felt under the bottom

75

cymbal. Some clutches and bottom cymbal holders have rubber alternatives for the old-fashioned felts. The harder the material and the smaller the contact area, the brighter the sound of your cymbals will be.

Drop-lock clutches

A variation on the regular hi-hat clutch is the so-called *drop-lock clutch*, a design for drummers with double bass drums or a double bass drum pedal. The drop-lock clutch allows you to release the top cymbal by hitting a special handle on the clutch. The cymbal drops onto the bottom cymbal so you can play the hi-hat with your sticks while using your hi-hat foot to play the secondary bass drum (pedal). Stepping on the hi-hat pedal just once is enough to make the drop-lock clutch pick up and 'lock' the top cymbal again.

Too loose

Using a drop-lock clutch, your 'closed' hi-hat will always sound a bit loose, as the top cymbal simply rests on the bottom one, rather than being pressed against it with a pedal. As an alternative, you can use an X-hat or a remote hi-hat (see the opposite page).

Locks and spurs

Memory locks are common on the upper tube of the hi-hat stand. Many hi-hats come with one or two spurs, or with Velcro if there's a base plate.

Swivel foot and two-legged hi-hats

A *swivel foot* allows you to swivel the legs around the base of the stand, which gives you additional flexibility in a setup with a double bass drum pedal, for example. As an alternative, there are hi-hat stands with just two legs, a base plate replacing the third leg. On some of these pedals, base plate and footboard can be folded up for transportation. If not, they take up a lot of space in your hardware case.

Remote pedals and X-hats

Want an extra pair of hi-hats? Two options: One is a *remote hi-hat pedal*, which is operated by means of a long cable, so you can

A two-legged
hi-hat (left),
a remote hi-hat
(lower right),
and an X-hat
(Axis – upper
right).

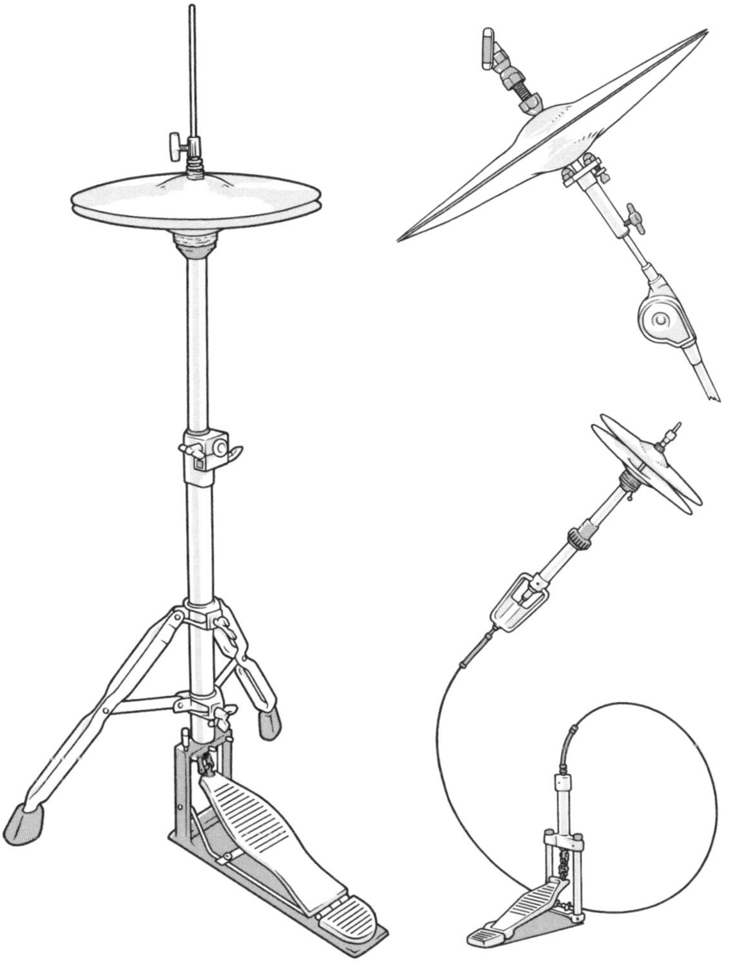

position the top section and the cymbals pretty much anywhere you like (somewhere over the first floor tom in most cases). The additional pedal is operated with the same foot as the regular hi-hat pedal.

Number two

Solution number two is an *X-hat* or *closed hat*, which comes without a pedal. An X-hat simply holds a pair of cymbals. Setting the tension of the built-in spring makes for tight or loose hi-hat sounds, or anything in between.

77

STANDS

Even the most basic stands usually do what they're supposed to do. Still, there are some things to check out.

Hardware.

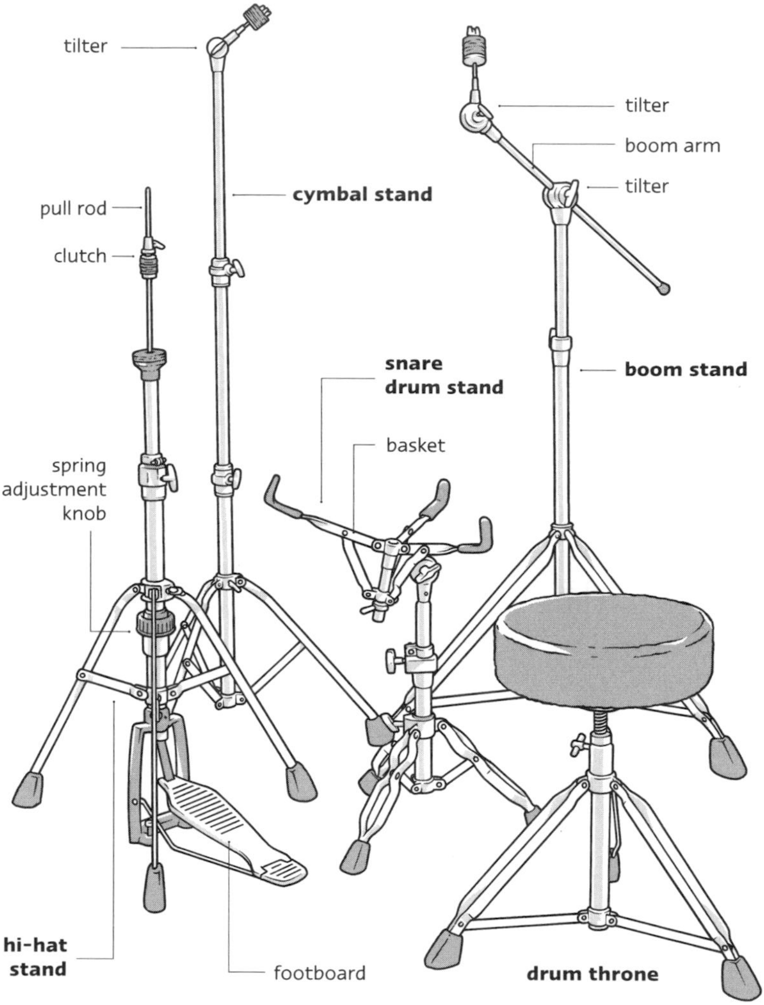

tilter — cymbal stand — pull rod — clutch — spring adjustment knob — snare drum stand — basket — boom stand — tilter — boom arm — tilter

hi-hat stand — footboard — **drum throne**

Double-braced legs
Many stands and hi-hat pedals come with double-braced legs, each leg consisting of two metal strips. This offers additional stability,

78

and double-braced stands are a lot heavier than their single-braced counterparts. Note that the latter may be all you need if you're not a real heavy hitter.

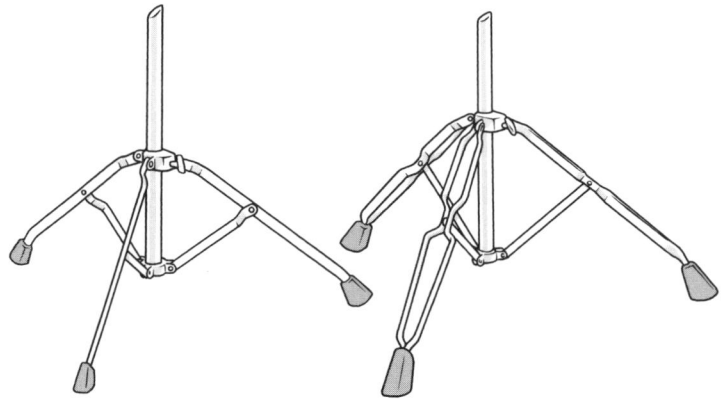

Single and double braced legs.

Fast
Some brands have stands with very 'fast' hose clamps; turning the wing nut just once is enough to tighten or loosen the clamp. Others take more turns, and thus more set-up and break-down time. When checking out stands, note that the tubes should telescope easily, and that the legs should fold in and out very easily.

TIP

Toothless tilters

As on tom holders, toothless tilters on cymbal stands offer infinite adjustment and are faster to work with than the traditional ratchet tilters, which have two sets of interlocking teeth. The finer the teeth, of course, the finer the adjustment will be. Ball-and-socket joints, as found on some snare stands, can be adjusted in any direction.

Pilot
On some stands, the stem of the cymbal tilter has an unthreaded top (known as a pilot). This pilot keeps the *cymbal retainer nut* from slipping off down when you try to fit it or remove it.

79

Retainer nut alternatives

There are various alternatives to the traditional cymbal retainer nut, ranging from sleeve/nut combinations (*e.g.*, Tama's Cymbal Mate) to T-tops. They save you set-up time and prevent you from tightening down cymbals too much (see also page 140).

Some alternatives to the traditional wing nut assembly.

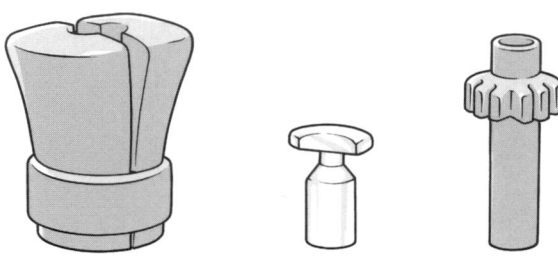

Boom stands

Some boom stands come with counterweights on the boom arm, but you usually do without this extra mass. When in doubt, think about acquiring a stand with a detachable counterweight. There are also convertible boom stands: If you don't need the boom arm, you can simply make it disappear into the stand's upper tube.

TIPCODE

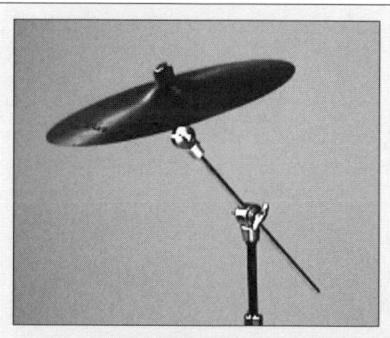

Tipcode DRUM-009
A brief demonstration of a convertible boom stand.

Securing the snare drum

A large (wing) nut secures the snare drum between the rubber grips of the snare drum stand basket. Some companies have designed a quick one-touch handle for this purpose. *Tip:* Tightening the basket too much may stifle the sound of the drum.

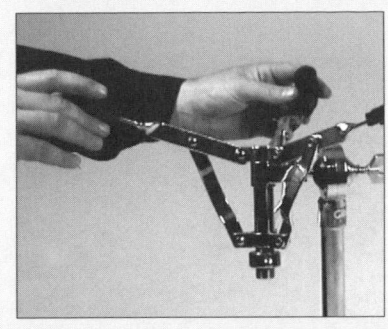

Tipcode DRUM-010
Securing a snare drum in a snare drum basket is shown in this Tipcode.

TIPCODE

Snare drum stand dimensions

Most snare drum stands hold 13" drums as easily as 14" ones, and some even take a 15" as easily as a 12". Also consider the maximum and minimum height settings of the stand, especially if it might be used for very deep or very shallow snare drums too.

Two parts

Some cheaper cymbal stands consist of two parts, rather than three. They have one potential drawback only: These parts need to be longer to reach a proper height, so they may not fit a hardware case or bag. Other than that, they can be just fine.

RACKS, CLAMPS AND THRONES

Drum racks help you to set up every item of your set, including microphones, in exactly the same position every time. They also clean up the look of your set, the usual forest of stands making way for three or four sturdy legs. Setting up can be a lot faster too. The bigger your set, the more useful a drum rack will be. For standard five-piece setups and for drummers who like to vary their setup from time to time and from gig to gig, traditional stands are usually more effective than drum racks.

Multi-clamps

Multi-clamps or adapters save floor space. They vary from very

81

Setup with drum rack.

basic affairs to clamps with multiple angling possibilities. The ones with hinge joints are the easiest to work with. Some clamps can hold thicker tubes only; others also hold rods.

Multi-clamps.

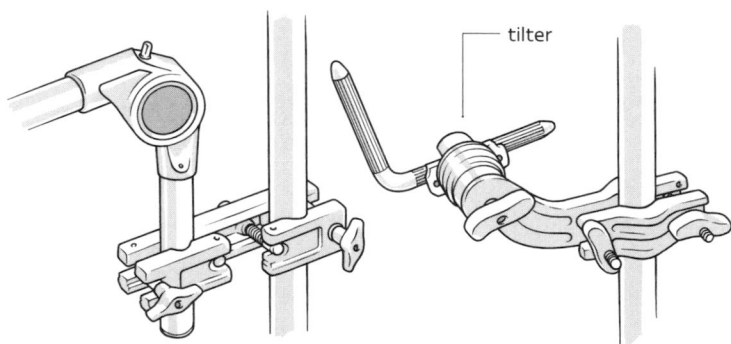

tilter

Thrones

If you can't set your throne to the exact height you need, or if it wobbles, chances are your back will tell you something's wrong after a few hours of drumming, or after just twenty minutes — or, more dangerously, after a couple of months. A good throne easily

82

costs somewhere between seventy-five and hundred fifty dollars. On the most basic ones, the height is set by inserting a bolt into either one of a series of holes in the center tube. If this doesn't allow for the exact height you want, simply drill an extra hole in the tube, or have someone do that for you. Other thrones have threaded rods, which allow for infinite height adjustment. Ideally, turning the seat should not alter its height.

The seat

Traditionally, drum thrones have rather small, round seats. Saddle-shaped seats may offer more comfort, as well as preventing the blood circulation in your upper legs from being cut off. Seats covered in fabric, instead of the usual vinyl, help prevent a sweaty feeling. A mesh seat is the best solution to fight the effects of excessive perspiration.

Hard or soft

Picking the right seat hardness is largely a matter of taste, and your own weight is another consideration. Softer seats may feel more comfortable at first, but a harder seat may offer better support in longer sessions. A back support (preferably adjustable) can be a welcome addition, especially when you have to play for hours on end.

7

Drum heads

Drum heads are the single most important element in the sound of your drums, so it's good to take a closer look at what's available — from single ply and two-ply heads to thin and self-muffled heads, and everything in between.

If you compare a drum set to a home stereo system, the drum heads correspond to the speakers. They are the elements that set the air in motion, and that's essentially what creates the sound that you hear.

The difference

With home stereo systems, it's usually much easier to hear the difference between two sets of speakers than it is to identify the difference between two amplifiers or CD players. Likewise, it is a lot easier to hear the difference between two identical drums with different heads and tunings, than it is to identify two different drums with the same heads and tunings.

The same drums, different sounds

Another example? It's easy to make three identical 12" toms sound completely different, simply by using different heads and tunings. A thin head and a high tuning will make it sound short, bright, and clear. A very low tuning and a two-ply head make for a fat, wet sound. And a medium head and tuning produces the fullest, longest and most 'musical' sound.

Different drums

Now take three different 12" toms, provide them with identical heads and tune them the same — and you'll see that telling them apart may be not that easy...

Budget heads?

Many budget sets come with budget heads that dent easily, are harder to tune, and don't sound good: They're not focused, for example, or their sound seems to be unbalanced no matter how good you are at drum tuning. Replacing these heads with professional quality drum heads will noticeably clear up the sound.

The most audible improvement usually comes from changing the batter heads of the toms, which will set you back some thirty-five to fifty dollars for the three of them. If you've got the cash, replace the snare drum batter as well, followed by the bass drum batter. It will make a difference — really. For total perfection, it's best to replace the resonant heads as well.

Medium

The most basic drum head consists of a clear, single ply of medium-heavy polyester film. This type of head — when tuned well — typically produces an open, even, true sound, with lots of sustain. It's very popular on toms, both top and bottom. Some examples of this type of head are the Remo Ambassador, the Evans G1, the Aquarian Classic Clear, and the Attack 1-ply Medium Clear.

Drum head material and thickness

Most drum heads use the same type of polyester film. It's generally referred to as Mylar, which is the trade name of one of its manufacturers (Dupont). Medium gauge drum heads basically all have the same thickness, often indicated as 1000 gauge or 1 mil., equal to 0.01" or 0.25 mm. Some types of film are softer than others, making for a mellower sound (and denting sooner than harder types of film!).

Medium coated

The most popular batter head for snare drums is a medium head with a white, somewhat coarse coating. This coating muffles the head ever so slightly, yet it seems also to produce a somewhat brighter or crisper attack. It also roughens the surface of the head, which is necessary if you want to use *wire brushes* (see pages 99–100). Medium coated heads are often used on toms and — less frequently — on bass drums too.

Two-ply

Heavier players often use two-ply batter heads, especially on their toms and bass drums. These heads sound fatter, warmer, and shorter than one-ply heads: The two-ply construction muffles lots of overtones.

Two-ply heads also last longer than single-ply heads. Some examples are Remo's Pinstripe, the Evans G2, Aquarian's Performance II, and the Attack Thin Skin 2-ply.

CHAPTER 7

No resonant heads

Don't use two-play heads as resonant heads, because this would kill the drum's projection. For toms, a popular combination is a two-ply on top and a single-ply medium or thin clear head on the bottom. Two-ply heads are usually made up of two 700-gauge plies, adding up to a total thickness of 0.36 mm.

Different types of heads.

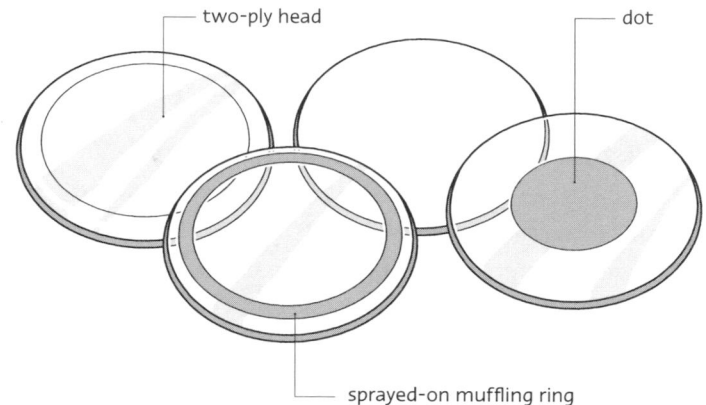

two-ply head · dot · sprayed-on muffling ring

Dots

If two-ply heads sound too muffled for your taste, you could consider dotted heads, which have an extra piece of drum head material in the middle of the head. These dots control the sound, making it slightly deeper and more focused, and they strengthen the head at the main point of impact. Traditional dotted heads are mostly used as tom batter heads. Because drum heads with regular dots are difficult to play with brushes, there are (coated) snare drum batter heads that have a dot on the reverse side.

Different heads and the types of drums with which they can be used.

drums	toms batter	toms resonant	snare batter	snare resonant	bass batter	bass front
head types						
transparent medium	●	●			●	●
coated medium	●	●	●		●	●
two-ply/dotted	●				●	●
thin		●				
built-in muffling ring			●		●	●
snare-side head				●		

TIPBOOK DRUMS

Thin
Thin single-ply heads are used primarily as resonant heads for toms. Combined with two-ply batter heads, these thin resonant heads increase the drum's projection and brightness. Most thin heads use 700 gauge or 0.18 mm film. If you do low-volume gigs only, you may of course consider using 700 gauge heads as batter heads: They will make for a very fast response.

Snare-side head
Snare drums need special *snare-side heads* or *snare heads*. These heads are extremely thin in order to allow the snares to bounce off the head and create the sound they're there for. Most medium snare-side heads are 300-gauge. Playing very quiet gigs only? Then try a 200-gauge model (only 0.05mm!). Heavy drummer? Go for 500 gauge. *Tip:* Never play the snare-side head. It dents really easily.

Muffling
Many drummers muffle their drum heads to help reduce overtones, making for a slightly fatter, mellower, drier sound. You can find various muffling techniques on pages 133–136. As an alternative, most drum head makers offer one or more series of self-muffled heads, i.c., drum heads with some type of built-in muffling, such as muffling rings, a splash of oil, a ridge, or tiny vent holes.

Removable rings
In the late 1990s the built-in *muffling ring* became increasingly popular on snare drum (batter head) and bass drum heads (both

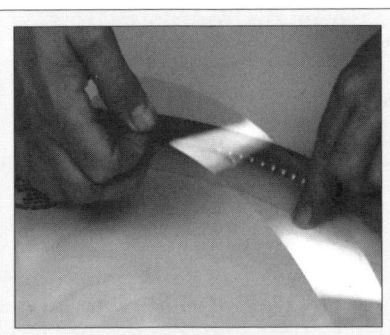

Tipcode DRUM-011
This Tipcode shows a bass drum head with a second, removable muffling ring.

TIPCODE

heads). These very thin rings, which float against the inside of the head, don't alter the attack sound because they bounce off the head as you strike it. The muffling effect follows the attack, slightly drying out and shortening the sound. Some self-muffled bass drum heads come with two rings, one of them removable. Sprayed-on muffling rings have a very, very slight effect on the sound.

Oil
The Evans Hydraulic heads have a touch of oil between their two plies. The oil makes for a very wet, fat, and controlled sound with an enhanced attack and a very short sustain. *Tip:* Other clear, two-ply heads may look as though they contain oil too. However, the 'oily' colors you see are usually the result a refraction of light, similar to what rainbows are generated by.

Ridges and holes
Also, there are drum heads with a ridge or a series of tiny holes around their circumference. Both features help control the drum's overtones. Of course, their effect is much more delicate than Evans' thin layer of oil, for example.

Calf skin
Various drum head makers produce one or more types of drum heads that are designed to recreate the warmer, softer feel and the more complex sound of calf skin heads. Why not use calf skin anymore? Because it's not as durable as plastic, and because calf skin drum heads are very sensitive to changes in temperature and humidity: You may have to tune them three or more times a night, especially if you have to bring your drums in from the cold.

Strong heads
Heavy hitter? Then you may want to experiment with special types of heads made of the same type of fibers that can be found in bullet proof vests (*i.e.*, Kevlar).

Two heads, one drum
Finding the right heads is a matter of experimentation, time, and patience. Comparing heads for toms? Take a tom. Put one head

on one side, the other on the other side, and tune them the to the same pitch. (This requires you to muffle one head as you tune and check the pitch of the other. If you don't, the heads will make you believe that they produce the same pitch even if they have different tunings!). The result will be not be the same as using a batter head with a dedicated resonant head, but you will be able to spot differences between the two batter heads.

Another brand

Changing your drum set may prompt you to change heads too, as some heads sound better than others on some sets. Don't limit yourself. Your toms may sound best with Brand A heads, while a Brand B batter head gets the best out of your bass drum, and your snare loves a Brand C on top. Also, similar head types from different brands will behave differently: A two-ply head from one brand may sound a lot warmer or brighter, or it may dent more or less easily than a similar head from another company. The exact type of film is one the elements that comes into play, of course.

Drum head brands

The four main drum head makers are Remo, Evans, Aquarian, and Attack. Two drum makers that have their own heads are Ludwig and RMV. Most other drum makers have their heads made by one the four major companies, or by Asian drum head makers. Budget sets typically come with anonymous, Asian-made drum heads featuring the drums' brand name.

8

Drum sticks

The number of drum sticks you can choose from is overwhelming. This chapter provides the know-how you need to make an informed choice when it comes to selecting your favorite tools. The best sticks you can get? The ones you don't even notice when you play...

Drum sticks come in hundreds of different sizes and types. Within all these variations, there are four basic types of drum sticks: the light and slim 7A, the versatile 5A and 5B, and the hefty 2B. Their details are shown in the chart on page 96.

Some basics

Whether you prefer heavier (usually thicker) or lighter (thinner) sticks depends on a number of things. Sound is one of them. Heavier sticks typically generate more low frequencies, producing a fuller, richer sound — at low volumes, too! Generally speaking, heavier drummers use heavier sticks for a heavier sound. Heavier cymbals require heavier sticks to get the extra bronze to move. Deeper drums (or drums with self-muffled heads) are typically played with heavier sticks, for pretty much the same reason: An instrument with a slower response responds better to a heavier stick. Conversely, heavy sticks are usually not the best choice if you play thin heads and cymbals: You could easily damage them.

Exceptions

At the same time, there are many exceptions to these rules. While playing softly is harder with heavier sticks, some drummers do so anyway: They simply prefer the full sound or the solid feel of a heavier, thicker stick. Also, there are drummers who manage to sound surprisingly heavy and big with surprisingly light sticks. And while most drummers always play with one and the same type of stick, others use different types of sticks for different gigs, different venues, or even for different songs.

For starters

Beginners will find it hard to appreciate the sometimes minute differences between the many different stick models available. It is a good idea to start with one of the standard models. This will generally be a 5A; for young players, a pair of 7As might be a better choice. Does a 5A feel too light to you, than try a pair of 5B sticks. 2B sticks are usually considered a bit too much for beginning players of any age or physique. Once you find out which one of these four types suits you best, you can 'fine-tune' your selection by going through the many variations that the various brands offer. Here are some guidelines.

94

The best sticks

The best sticks are the ones that make you feel, play and sound the way you like it. More importantly, they're the sticks you don't really notice when you play. A pair of sticks shouldn't feel good, some say: You should not feel them at all...

The differences

Sticks basically differ in thickness, length, weight, and balance. A thicker stick will feel 'meatier' in your hand, and it produces a meatier sound. The longer a stick is, the easier it goes down (good for playing loud), but the slower it comes up (bad for playing fast). Also, a longer stick provides you with more reach. Of course, both length and thickness of a stick influence its weight.

Balance

The balance of a stick has to do with its weight distribution. A short taper and a thick neck move the weight forward, making the stick feel and sound heavier than it actually is, and vice versa. Whether a stick has the 'right' balance largely depends on where you hold it (at the far end, of more towards the middle) and the exact technique you use.

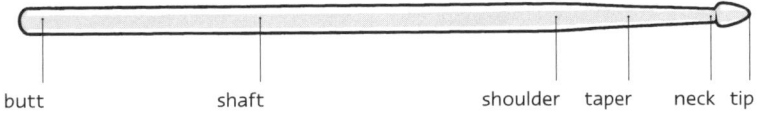

butt   shaft   shoulder   taper   neck tip

Not the same

The 'standard' types of sticks (5A, 5B, 7A, 2B) are not exactly standard: Every drum stick maker has different ideas of what these 'standard' sticks should be. Still, all 5As of different brands have at least a few things in common, and the same goes for the other standard types from different companies. The following chart shows the average dimensions of these four types of stick. The same chart works well as a point of reference for any other type of stick.

95

type	weight	length	diameter	neck
7A	45 grams	15.75"/40 cm	0.530"/13.5 mm	0.235"/6 mm
5A	50 grams	16"/40.5 cm	0.570"/14.5 mm	0.255"/6.5 mm
5B	55 grams	16"/40.5 cm	0.610"/15.5 mm	0.275"/7 mm
2B	65 grams	16.25"/41 cm	0.640"/16.5 mm	0.295"/7.5 mm

Feels like more

As you can see, everything increases just a little at a time, yet a 2B feels very (very!) different from a 7A — which also explains the astounding number of models available. Sometimes 'Rock' and 'Jazz' are regarded as standard models too, but the variations in their specifications from one brand to another are much bigger than those in the four standard types listed:. The Rock type sold by one brand may be as much as 1.5 times heavier than the next brand's Rock stick.

TIP

Letters

The letters in 7A en 2B go back to the early 20th century. The A in 7A or 5A indicates these models were designed as 'All-purpose' sticks; the B in 2B refers to the word 'Band', and the letter S — rare, among sticks for drum set drummers — stands for 'Snare'

Hickory, maple, oak

The weight, feel, and sound of a pair of sticks are also influenced by the type of wood. Most sticks are made of hickory, a dense, heavy, strong, yet flexible type of wood. It has good shock absorption (which explains why it's also used for hammer and pick handles, for example), reducing fatigue and the risk of injuries. Maple sticks weigh much less than hickory sticks of the same model, making for a lighter sound.

- You like the feel, but not the weight of a thick stick? Try a similar model in maple.

- You like the weight of a stick, but it's too thin for your taste?

96

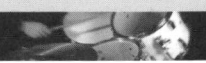

Again, try a similar model in maple.

- Heavy hitter? Try oak. It's heavy, dense and strong, promoting a bright and well-defined sound.

The tip

The *bead* or *tip* of a stick is important for the sound. This goes both for its material and for its exact size and shape. Most sticks come with wooden tips. Nylon tips, a popular alternative, last much longer and sound a lot brighter. If you want to fully appreciate the difference, play a ride cymbal with various wooden and nylon tipped drum sticks.

Tip size

Tip shape and size help determine the sound your sticks produce. Again, these differences are best heard on cymbals. Bigger tips make for a bigger, fuller sound by generating more highs and lows. Small tips yield a very controlled sound. The smaller the tip, the easier your sticks will dent your heads, unless you're not a heavy hitter.

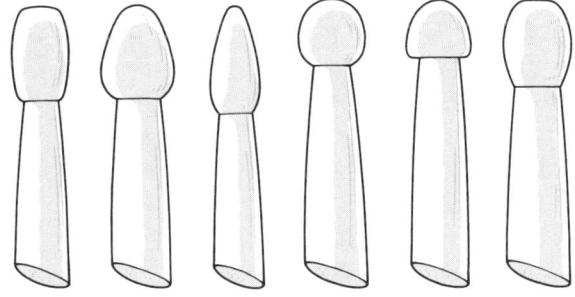

Every tip gives a different sound.

Tip shape

The shape of the tip influences the sound the sticks produce. Examples of tip shapes include ball-shaped tips (round, spherical tip; well defined, articulate sound), barrel tips (lots of punch and power), teardrop tips (dark, low, rich), acorn-shaped tips (pointed oval; full sound), ellipse tips (focused), mushroom, and oval or olive-shaped tips. Oval tips offer the largest range of sound variations on your ride cymbal: Changing the angle at which you play the cymbal immediately alters the sound.

97

Different or identical tips

Most stick manufacturers offer distinctive shapes for nylon and wood tips on their otherwise identical models. Others have identical nylon and wood tips for each separate stick model they make.

Finish

Most sticks have a lacquer or wax finish. How these finishes feel is very personal, depending largely on your type of sweat and your skin. A stick that becomes slippery in your hands may feel great in the hands of another drummer. There are also differences between various types of lacquers or waxes, of course.

Get a grip

Slippery sticks? You can try a similar stick with a different coating (*i.e.*, from another brand), try playing with drummers' gloves, wrap your sticks with commercially available stick tape. Also available are grip enhancing powders that you apply to your fingers. Some alternative solutions? Unfinished sticks, sticks with knurled grips, sticks with built-in rubber grips, sticks with thicker grip areas...

Vibration reduction

When playing relatively hard surfaces such as rubber pads (practice pads, electronic drum pads), sticks tend to vibrate in a way that can be quite tiring. Some sticks have a vibration-reducing design to counteract the effect.

Equal weight, equal sound

Most drummers look for a pair of sticks that are equal in weight and sound. Some brands offer computer-selected pairs that are matched extremely well — but even then you may still want to select a few pairs that all have a similar weight and sound.

Checks

Checking for straightness? Roll the sticks over the counter. Checking for sound? Play them one by one on a wooden counter or tabletop, or use one stick to play the other. Some drummers even play their heads — the one on their shoulders — to find sticks that produce the same pitches.

Weight differences

Not many drum stores have a postal scale, though such a device speeds up the process if you want to select a larger number of sticks that all weigh the same. A basic rule of thumb: If you can't feel the weight difference in the store, you probably won't feel it when you play. 'Identical' sticks, whether pre-packed or not, easily vary 10% or more in weight — and that you can feel.

Non-wood

There are various types of non-wood sticks available, such as synthetic sticks, carbon fiber sticks, or metal sticks with a plastic cover. These sticks typically last longer than wooden sticks, they're consistent in terms of weight and balance, they don't splinter, and they're basically always straight. Some of them sound pretty or very close to (nylon-tipped) wooden sticks; others sound quite different, even on drums. Prices range from some fifteen to more than thirty dollars. Brands include Ahead, Carbosticks, Duratech, and Techra.

Wire brushes

Drummers play with more than just sticks. *Wire brushes*, for instance, are mainly used by jazz drummers. The most common wire brushes have retractable steel wires, a rubber grip, and a loop end that allows for a variety of sounds and effects, especially on cymbals.

Gauges and handles

Wire brushes, usually just called *brushes*, differ in the exact gauge of wire (a heavier gauge producing a heavier, broader, coarser sound), in the wire material (steel has a more refined, subtle sound than nylon), and in the material of the handle (rubber coated, wood, plastic, or plain metal), as well as in balance and weight. Wire brushes with rubber coated handles are the most popular choice, even though the rubber may become a bit sticky after playing a while. Brushes typically cost between fifteen and forty dollars a pair.

99

Telescopic brushes.

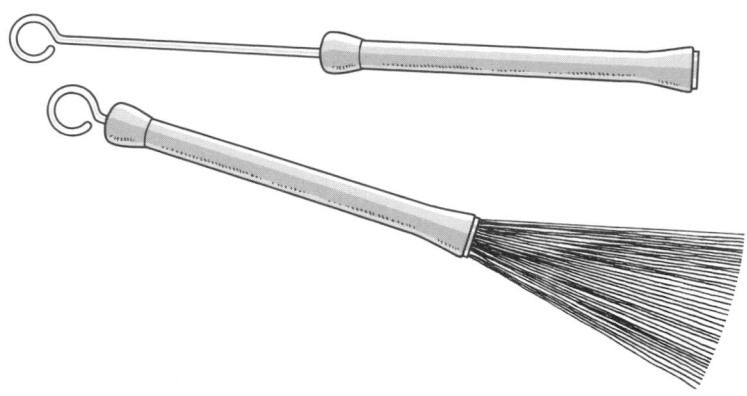

Multi-rods

You can also use tightly bundled wooden or plastic dowels, commonly known as *multi-rods*. They produce sounds somewhere between sticks and brushes. Multi-rods come in many varieties, with more or fewer dowels, heavier or lighter dowels, and so on. On some types, the sound can be influenced by moving a plastic collar up or down the dowels. A tip: Though multi-rods are often suggested to be great for low-volume gigs, they do not always sound good when playing them softly — and you can play really softly with sticks too!

Multi-rods

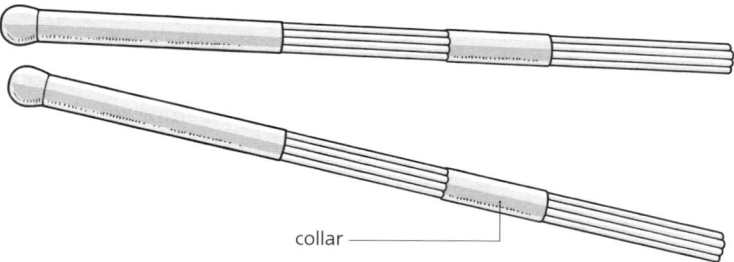

collar

Mallets

You can also play your drums and cymbals with *mallets*. Mallets come in many different types, typically with a thin shaft and a relatively large, round head; they're used to play *mallet instruments* (see pages 154–155).

The types that are best suited for drums and cymbals have a *wrapped head*: The head is wrapped with yarn or cord, for example.

100

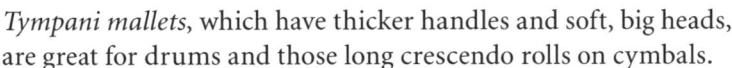
Tympani mallets, which have thicker handles and soft, big heads, are great for drums and those long crescendo rolls on cymbals.

Brands

Some of the established manufacturers in this area are Pro-Mark, Regal Tip, Vater, Vic Firth, and Zildjian, every one of them producing dozens of different models. Other makers include Hornets, Hot Sticks, Pellwood, Silver Fox, Shaw, and Trueline. Some stick makers produce sticks for other companies as well. This explains why you may come across two identical sticks with different brand names.

9

Cymbals

Cymbals look very simple, but they're not. They're quite complex instruments, actually. Some basic knowledge on the subject will help you choose the cymbals that sound the way you like them to.

Finding the cymbals you like is easier if you know a little about why they sound the way they do. If you plan to use your ears only, you may skip to the tips on page 112.

Series

All larger cymbal makers produce cymbals in various price ranges, and most cymbal makers have at least a few professional series with distinctive sound characteristics, and often one or more series of cymbals that are specifically aimed at certain styles of music. Cymbal catalogs and cymbal makers' websites help you get a picture of what's available — and you may need some help indeed, with a choice of some three to four thousand cymbal models.

Clear names

Many cymbals have names that may help you make a first selection. Terms such as Power, Full, Dark, and Fast speak for themselves, more or less. Weight indications, such as Medium, aren't as straightforward as they appear: If you compare ten 16" Medium crash cymbals of various brands and series, you'll hear ten quite different cymbals — if only because the term 'Medium' is not standardized at all: A 16" medium crash of one brand may be no less than 20% lighter than a 'similar' cymbal of another company.

Heavier, larger, higher

The exact sound of a cymbal is the complex result of various interrelated elements. Four of them are quite straightforward, or so they appear: weight, diameter, profile, and cup size.

- If you had two identical cymbals, one slightly heavier than the other, the latter would sound both higher and longer. It would also have a slower response; in other words, a heavy crash needs quite a heavy blow to really crash.

- A larger cymbal has a lower pitch and a longer sustain than a similar but smaller cymbal. The larger cymbal also needs more power to be able to respond.

- Cup size influences volume, response, and the amount of overtones, which makes for a richer sound. A larger cup or bell makes a cymbal respond faster and produce a louder, more full-bodied sound.

- A cymbal with a higher bow will have a higher pitch and a slower response than the same cymbal with a flatter profile.

Interrelated

All these parameters are strongly interrelated — for instance, a heavier cymbal may sound lower than a lighter one of the same size because it has a lower profile.

Hammer marks

The way a cymbal has been worked also has an effect on the sound. The hammering, for instance: The more regular the pattern of hammer marks (the dents on the surface of the cymbal), the more 'regular' and cleaner the sound will be. An irregular pattern, such as created when hammering a cymbal by hand, helps produce a darker and more complex, 'irregular' sound.

Grooves

The circular grooves that most cymbals have enhance the spread of the sound. Cymbals that have no grooves (*unlathed cymbals*; see Chapter 14) have a tighter, drier, more compact, more metallic sound. Even, regular grooves promote an even, 'regular' or clean sound. Uneven grooves enhance the complex character of many hand-made cymbals.

Tipcode DRUM-012
Here's the visible difference between unlathed and lathed cymbals.

TIPCODE

Alloys

As a cymbal consists of one part only (the cymbal itself!), the material plays a major role in determining the sound. The following basic alloys are used in cymbal production:

105

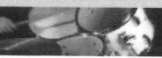

- The oldest alloy is a bronze containing 20% tin and 80% copper. This metal, known as **B20**, is mostly used for professional series by Zildjian, Sabian, UFIP, and most Turkish and Chinese cymbal companies.

- The lower tin content of **B8** (8% tin) gives this bronze alloy a slightly different look. Its somewhat tighter sound can be heard in cymbals such as the classic Paiste 2002s, in most professional Meinl cymbals, and in many lower and mid-range series of other brands.

- Budget cymbals can also be made of **brass** or **nickel-silver**, the first producing a warmer sound than the second.

- A growing number of (mainly medium budget) cymbals uses **B10** or **B12**, an alloy that is generally said to make for a slightly warmer sound than B8.

- Paiste's own **Sound Alloy** is closer to B20 than to B8.

'Identical' cymbals

Two cymbals of the same series, model, and size may still sound very different. These variations between 'identical' cymbals are generally greater if:

- they have an irregular hammering pattern. This promotes larger variations from one cymbal to another of the same series, model and size;

- they're made of B20. This alloy typically helps produce a wider frequency range than other alloys. The higher the number of different frequencies in a cymbal, the larger differences in sound will be.

In other words, even if you're sold on one particular type of cymbal, listen to and compare several samples of that particular cymbal model before deciding which one to buy — especially if you're dealing with hand-hammered B20 cymbals.

Budget cymbals

Cymbals often come in pre-packed sets, especially but not exclusively in lower price ranges. If you want to be sure that you'll

enjoy your purchase for a long time, unpack the set, and play-test each cymbal. There are major sound differences between low-budget series too, so you may very well enjoy the ride cymbal from one brand or series and the crash from another. Buying separate cymbals will be more expensive, though, even within the same series.

RIDE CYMBALS

The attack sound of a ride, the *ping*, may vary from a very penetrating, clean sound to something rather dark, thick, and dry. Generally speaking, louder music demands a more definite ping (more definition, that is) and a more cutting sound, which you'll get best from a heavier cymbal. A good test is to crash the cymbal and then play a ride beat at the volume you intend to use the cymbal. If you hear the individual beats from the very start, you're on the right track. Listen to the sound of the ping, which may range from high to low, dry to wet, thick to thin, solid to delicate, mean to friendly, or modest to provocative.

The cup
A ride cymbals' cup typically has a very tight, pronounced tone. However, it shouldn't sound as if you are playing a different cymbal when compared with the sound you get from the rest of

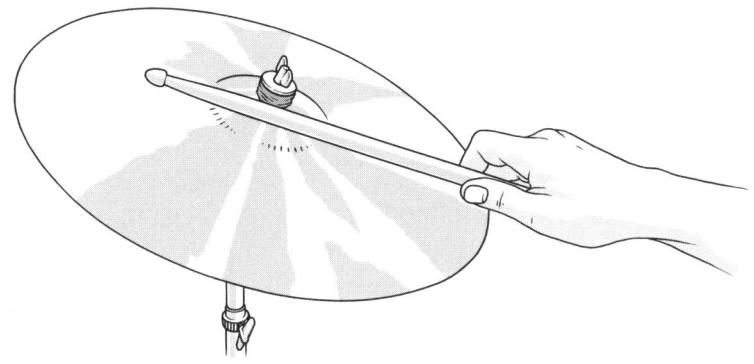

... the sound of the cup...

107

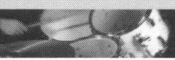

the cymbal. Also listen to what the rest of the cymbal does, when playing the cup. Does it start to sound along with the cup right away, or is it only the cup that you hear, no matter how hard you play it?

Crash-ride
Many 18" and bigger cymbals can be used for riding and crashing, and dedicated *crash-ride cymbals* are also available. Such cymbals can be a solution if you can afford only one cymbal. Professional crash-ride cymbals are rare. Many jazz and fusion drummers use their cymbals for riding as well as for crashing, choosing relatively thin cymbals with an irregular hammering, which produce a wide array of overtones or *harmonics*, as well as having sufficient definition to be used for ride patterns. These cymbals are usually not marketed as crash-ride cymbals, however.

Ride sizes
Most drummers use a 20" or 22" ride cymbal, but you can get them in 18", 19", and 21" as well. Smaller and bigger rides are rare.

Flat rides
Flat rides, which produce a delicate, very controlled ride sound, have no cup at all.

HI-HAT CYMBALS

When checking out hi-hat cymbals, play them in every way you're going to use them. Depressing the pedal should produce a good, definite *chick* sound. If it's followed by a sweeping tone, don't buy the cymbals. Playing them in closed position should produce a nice, tight sound. If they sound hollow, forget them. Open the hi-hats and play them with sticks, and see how fast they respond. Testing and comparing hi-hat cymbals is easiest if you have a few clutches at hand, so you can switch cymbals quickly and compare. Better still, use a couple of hi-hat stands, one for each pair of cymbals you're comparing.

Heavy bottom

If you need your hi-hats to produce a very definite chick sound, go for pairs that have a considerably heavier bottom cymbal. Loud drummers use both heavy top and bottom cymbals. Don't hesitate to mix tops and bottoms from various pairs, if the store owner allows you to do so.
Cymbal fanatics sometimes even end up mixing cymbals from different series, or brands.

Air-lock

To prevent air-lock (see page 75), various brands make bottom cymbals with corrugated edges or one or more additional holes in the bottom cymbal. Both features allow the air to escape from between the cymbals.

Hi-hat sizes

Most drummers use 14" hi-hats; others go for a pair of 13" hi-hats, which typically produce a higher pitch and a somewhat tighter sound. Even smaller sets, such as 10" and 12" hi-hats, are mainly used as additional hi-hats on an X-hat or a remote hi-hat (see pages 76–77). Larger hi-hats are rare.

CRASH CYMBALS

Some drummers like crashes that cut through everything. Others prefer them to disappear right after the attack, or they want them to sound as wet and warm as a hot shower. The most important thing is that a crash cymbal should be able to immediately produce its entire frequency range — from low to high — when you play it as softly as you will onstage.

Store versus stage

In the store, crashes always seem to sound longer than they will in real life. The louder the music you play, the larger this difference will be. A crash cymbal that seems to sound forever in the store, will sound a lot shorter onstage.

109

Too thin

Drummers with a heavy attack sometimes tend to buy crashes that are too thin for the music they play, because in the store thinner crashes are more pleasing to the ear than the cutting power crashes they actually need.

> ### Different
>
> *At a distance, when used in a band, crashes tend to sound much more alike than they do in the store. So go for extremes in contrast, but make sure the cymbals you play sound as a set as well.*

Crash sizes

Apart from 16" and 18" crashes, the most popular choices in any style, there are crashes in even and uneven sizes from 12" up to 22".

EFFECT CYMBALS

There's a wide range of so-called effect cymbals, such as Chinas and splashes, as well as a host of other variations.

Splashes

Splashes are basically small, thin, and therefore very fast crashes, with sizes from 6" to 12". Heavier splashes will not splash unless they're hit extremely hard. Really thin ones respond real fast — and if you play them real hard, they'll break real fast too.

Chinas and China types

Chinese cymbals were originally made to scare the enemy, and they still tend to scare fellow musicians who come too close. The upturned edge is one of the reasons for their aggressive, rough and exotic type of sound. The Western variations on this theme, with

110

a regular (so-called Turkish) cup often sound mellower, or less 'dirty' than the very affordable, but also more vulnerable cymbals from China.

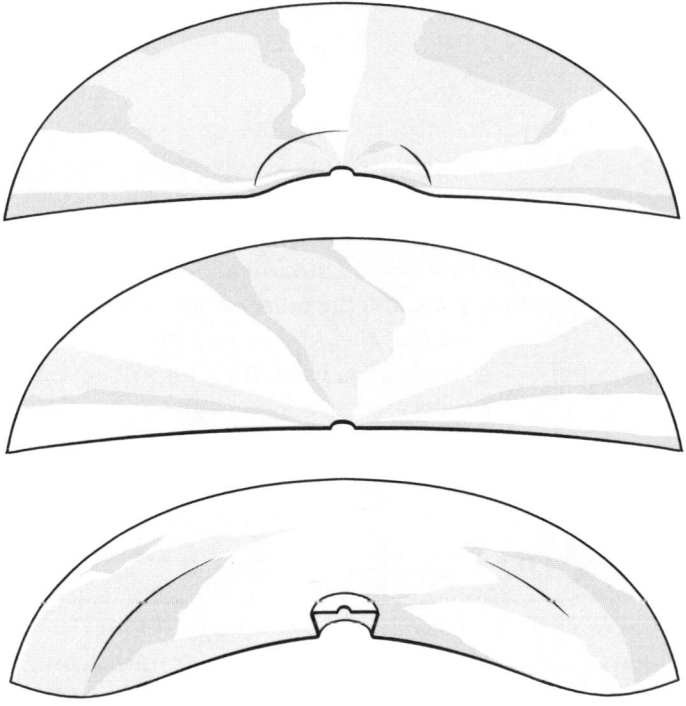

The profiles of a regular cymbal, a flat ride and an original Chinese cymbal.

Up or down

China cymbals can be mounted facing up or down. If you play one facing up, you have easy access to the cup, the bow, and the edge of the cymbal. Mounting it face down will typically promote darker tones, and it allows you to use the flange for a complex, explosive ride sound.

And more...

There are special cymbals for percussionists, and cymbals that are no more than a big cup, China splashes, cymbals with square cups, hexagonal cymbals, cymbals with jingles, cymbals with larger or smaller cut outs, cymbals that look like they were run over by a truck or two, and much more.

111

Sizzle cymbals

Sizzle cymbals, as their name suggests, make a sizzling sound. This effect is typically produced by two or more rivets, positioned near the cymbal's edge. Sizzle cymbals are mostly used by jazz drummers.

Sizzlers

If you want to experiment with this sound, or if you want to use it from time to time only, get a commercially available sizzler: a beaded chain that rests on the cymbal, vibrating along as you play it. No holes to be drilled! Alternatively, you can take a dime and stick it to the cymbal with a small piece of adhesive tape. Stick one end of the tape on the coin, and the other on the cymbal, allowing the coin to vibrate as you play the cymbal. Experiment with placement until you like what you hear. The coin will not produce the subtle sound that rivets typically do, though.

LISTEN UP

• If you're a first-time buyer, start by picking a **ride or the hi-hats**, depending on what you use most for timekeeping. Then find crashes, splashes, and effect cymbals to match your ride and/or hi-hat sound.

• If you're about to replace or add cymbals, take **the cymbals you already have** with you, so you can hear whether the new ones 'fit in'. A tip: Cymbal setups can include as many brands or series as you like.

• When play-testing cymbals, use **your own sticks** or a similar pair.

• When comparing cymbals, never listen to more than **three cymbals** at a time. Replace the one you like least with a similar cymbal. Listen. Replace the one you like least from the current trio. And so on.

• If possible, listen to your final selection **at a drum set**, so you can use them the way you do when you play.

- Bring **another drummer** along. Have him or her play so you can listen at a distance, and vice versa.

- No other drummer around? Close the **one ear** that's in the general direction of the cymbals, and play them; this will give you some idea of what the cymbals sound like 'live', in a band setting.

- The **ultimate test**? Use the cymbal in your band. Most shopkeepers won't let you, though, for obvious reasons.

Secondhand cymbals

There are plenty of used ride and hi-hat cymbals for sale. After all, they hardly ever break, they're quite expensive, and many drummers tend to go for a change from time to time. Pre-owned splashes and crashes are quite rare. A few tips.

- **Cracked cymbals** will invariably crack further. Don't buy them.

- Check used cymbals for **invisible cracks**. Play the edge of the cymbal with your finger or a soft mallet, hold the cymbal close to your ear and listen for the slightest buzzing or rattling.

- Avoid cymbals with a **worn-out hole** (known as a *key hole*); they have been played without a cymbal sleeve (see page 139).

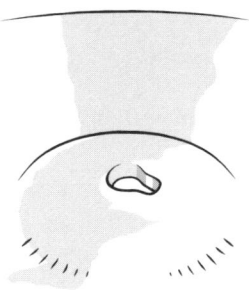

A cymbal with a worn-out key hole.

- Cymbals that shine very **brightly around the hole** have probably been mounted too tight, which increases the risk of cracking.

- Other than that: Please enjoy your used cymbals as much as if you'd bought them new. They can last for decades. Splashes,

113

too. Some drummers even prefer **old cymbals** (especially the famous and rare old Ks from the formerly Turkish Zildjian factory). They're so popular, in fact, that most brands offer special series to recreate the cymbal sounds of the 1950s and 1960s, with names like Traditional, Original, Classic, Nostalgia, or Constantinople (the former name of Istanbul).

10

Tuning and muffling

Unlike most other instruments, drums can't sound out of tune. So why tune them? To make sure they sound as good as they can, and to make sure they sound the way you want them to. It takes seconds to make a set of great drums sound like boxes. It takes quite a bit longer to tune them to their best. The basics are set out in this chapter, which also includes tips on muffling.

It's up to you how you want to tune your drums — high and tight, or wet and fat, or anywhere in between. Every drum has a certain range it can be tuned to. Tuning it higher will make it choke; tuning it too low kills the tone and renders it unplayable. In either case you will get a lot of attack and very little or no tone or sustain.

In the middle

Every drum can also be tuned to a point, somewhere in between these extremes, at which each element of the instrument seems to come together. When you tune it to that pitch, you'll hear the longest, fullest, biggest, and most musical tone that the drum is capable of producing. A tip in advance: Learning to tune drums takes time and lots of practice, so be patient.

One per string

Tuning a guitar is quite easy. There's just one tuning mechanism for each string. Each string can be tuned either too low (*flat*), too high (*sharp*), or just right.

Five or more per head

Tuning drums is quite a bit harder, as there are five to ten tension rods for each drum head. Properly tuning a head means creating an even tension at each rod. One of the things that makes drum tuning quite hard, is that adjusting one rod also influences the tension at the other rods.

The drum and the set

Tuning a drum set requires not only that each head has an even tension all around, making it in tune with itself, but also that there's a balance between the top and bottom heads of each drum. Finally, tuning a drum set also includes tuning the drums relative to each other, creating the *intervals* (the pitch distances from drum to drum) that you like.

12", 13", 16"

The sizes of the drums dictate these intervals to some extent. If you have 12", 12" and 16" toms, there will be a large interval between the 13" and the 16". You can try to make this interval smaller by tuning the 13" quite low and the 16" quite high — but this will result in two drums that do not sound like they're parts of the same instrument: The low tuning on the 13" will make it sound fat, while a high tuning on a 16" easily makes for a thin, and possibly even choked sound.

Drum keys

Pretty much every brand has its own model of *drum key*, but every key fits every drum (except for older Sonor drums that often use slotted tension rods). Most drum keys have a hole that allows you to attach them to a key chain.

Speed keys and ratchet keys

Apart from regular drum keys, there are various types of keys that help you tune or remove heads faster, such as *speed keys* and *ratchet keys*.

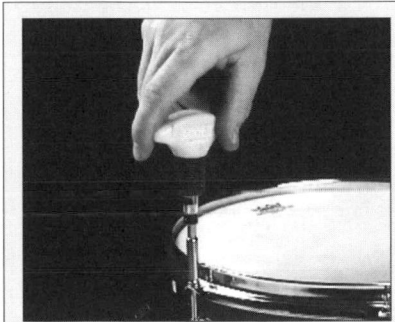

Tipcode Drum-013
A demonstration of the ease of use of a ratchet key.

 **TIPCODE**

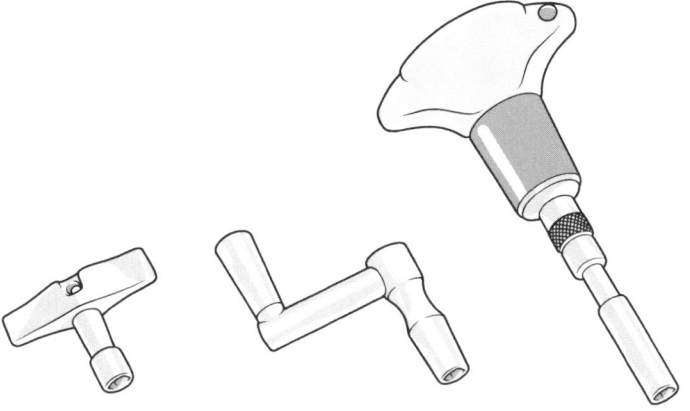

A regular drum key, a speed key, and a ratchet key.

117

BASIC TUNING

To get most from the following section, preferably use a 12" or a 13" tom, as they're easier to handle than a floor tom, and easier to tune than most 10" toms. Remove both heads. *Tip:* To do so in no time, try using two drum keys simultaneously (see Tipcode Drum–014, next page!). Put the drum on a folded towel or a piece of foam plastic so you don't damage its bearing edge.

Dented or stretched

Replace the heads as soon as they're dented or stretched. You can easily tell a stretched head: Take it off and look at it from the side. A sagging head has lost most of its elasticity and therefore most of its sound. This goes for bottom heads too! You don't play these heads, of course, but you will find that you have to tune them up over time, which indicates that they do stretch — ever so slowly.

TIP

Time for cleaning

While the heads are off, you may want to clean the hoops, the inside of the drum, the lugs, and the rods, and check the bearing edge.

A new and a worn-out drum head.

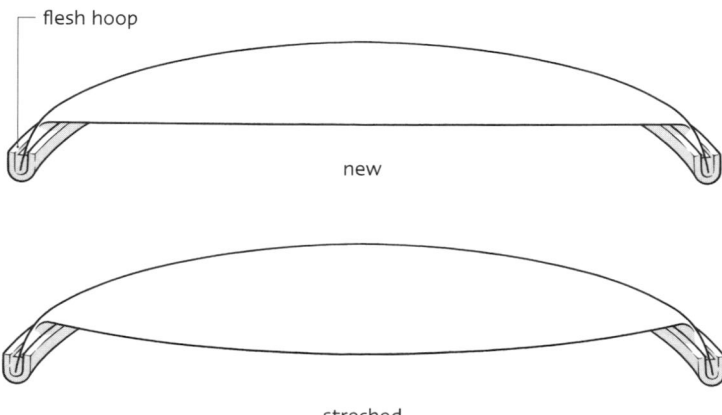

flesh hoop

new

streched

Basic tension

Put the batter head on the drum. To create a basic even tension all around the head, use your fingers to tighten all the tension rods as well as you can. This may be hard, for instance if there's not too much room between the lug casings and the counter hoop. If so, use a drum key to turn each rod so that the underside of its head just touches the counter hoop.

Tipcode Drum-014
It takes a bit of practice, but you can loosen or tighten two tension rods at the same time, as shown in this Tipcode.

TIPCODE

Tipcode Drum-015 and 016
This Tipcode shows you how to put the head on the drum (tip: Align the drum head logo with the drum's badge!). Use your fingers to create a basic even tension all around the head. The next step, increasing the tension with a drum key, is shown in Tipcode DRUM-016.

TIPCODE

Two by two

You can speed things up by using two keys, always loosening or tightening opposite rods simultaneously. On a drum with six tension rods per head, start with 1 and 2, then 3 and 4, and end with 5 and 6. The lug numbers are shown on the next page.

Higher and higher

Now slowly increase the tension, half a turn per rod at a time, following the illustrated order of lugs or any of the many

variations. When the head starts to produce an agreeable tone, you're nearly there.

The pitch

Continue tightening the rods, perhaps in quarter turns now. Meanwhile, lightly tap the head at each rod, about an inch from the edge, with your drum key, a fingertip, or a stick. As soon as you start hearing the pitch you're looking for, it's time for the hard part: fine-tuning. Fine-tuning is all about making sure the head produces the same pitch all around, at every tension rod.

Tuning order.

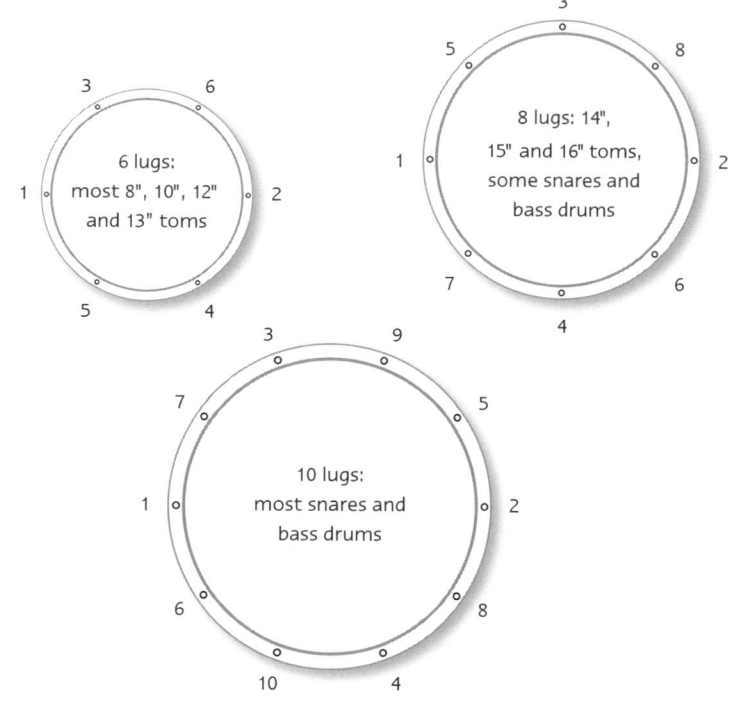

FINE-TUNING

No matter how precisely you've tuned this head so far, you'll find that it produces a slightly different pitch at each rod. To even that out and create an even tension and pitch all around takes time. Here are a few important tips.

- Defining the pitch is easier if you gently place **a finger in the exact center of the head**. Just touch it, don't push. Tapping at the lugs will now produce a clearer tone. (How come? Your finger muffles the drum head's fundamental tone, stressing the harmonics that are produced. Fine-tuning is all about balancing out these harmonics or overtones.)

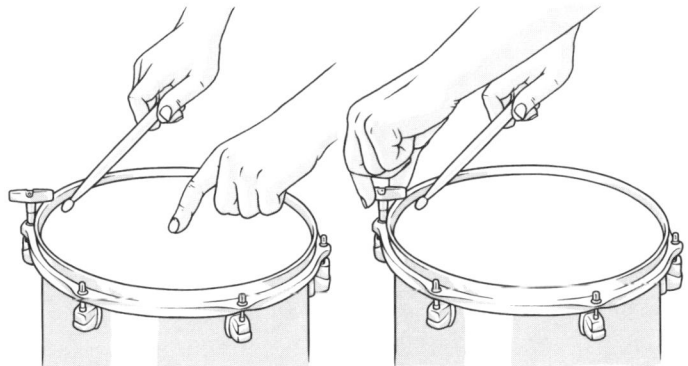

Placing a finger in the middle of the head, tapping, and adjusting the relevant tension rods.

- Take as your **starting point** the one rod at which you best like the pitch; this is now lug number 1. The pitch will probably be the same at the opposite lug, which becomes lug number 2.

- Compare this pitch to what you hear at lugs 3 and 4. If they sound too low (flat), tighten them a little. Note that the pitch at 1 and 2 goes up when doing this, so loosen them up a tiny bit. Drum tuning is about **creating a balance**: Give a little here, take a little there…

- Adjust all the key rods until the tension (and the pitch) is **even all around**. This sounds easier than it is. Why? An example: The pitch at opposite lugs often sounds identical — but that doesn't mean the tension is the same at those lugs. This may be the problem if, for example, you don't succeed in getting 3 and 4 to sound the same pitch as 1 and 2. If so, try tightening 2 and lowering the tension at 1, or the other way around. If that doesn't work, try the same with 3 and 4 (and so on).

- When comparing two pairs of rods, also **listen to the pitch at the other rods** from time to time. If the tension at 5 is much too low, on an eight-lug drum, you'll never get 1 and 3 to sound the same.

121

- If you want to **lower the pitch** at a certain lug, then don't just release it. Instead, always tune up: First, loosen the tension rod until the pitch is clearly too low, then go up from there.

- Can't manage? **Don't panic**. Take the heads off and start all over, either at once, or after taking a break, and consider asking an experienced drummer or your teacher to help you.

- **Practice, practice, practice**. Thousands of drummers play a reasonably well-tuned drum because they're afraid it will sound worse if they try to retune it. And it may indeed sound worse at first — until you've learnt how to properly tune your instrument.

Tipcode Drum-017

Here's an essential tip to help you determine the exact pitch of a drum head at each tension rod: Gently place a finger in the exact center of the head.

Three options

If your batter head has the pitch you want, mount the bottom head. Basically, you have three tuning options: Tune it to the same pitch as the batter head, to a higher pitch, or to a lower one.

1. Tuning the heads to the same pitch promotes a long, clear, clean, and even tone.
2. A higher-sounding bottom head will make for a tone that's brighter and livelier, with increased cut and projection.
3. Tuning your bottom head lower will result in a deeper sound — more of a thud, with reduced sustain. The tighter top head helps the stick rebound and accents the attack.

122

- A retrofittable **one-touch tuning system** that allows you to tune a drum with just one adjustment per head was introduced in 2007.

Tips
The only way to find out what you (or your drums) like best is to try each option. Here are some tips.

- **Don't overdo** the pitch difference between top and bottom heads.

- A different tuning for top and bottom produces a **pitch bend** effect: The pitch drops or goes up after the attack.

- Some drummers describe option 2 as a big, fat sound. Others use those words for option 3. Both groups agree that there's a **big difference** between 2 and 3…

- If your 12" tom has a tighter top head and your 10" has a tighter bottom head, these drums will not sound as if they're **part of the same instrument**. As a starting point, make sure that pitch relations between top and batter heads are the same for all of your rack toms and floor toms. Snare drums and bass drums are different!

Muffle the other head
When fine-tuning a head, always muffle the opposite head. Put the drum on your drum seat, or on a folded towel, for example. Also, when comparing the pitches of batter and bottom head, always muffle the other head. If not, both heads will sound similar, even when they're not tuned the same: Their pitches will tend to blend and sound like one.

Mounting the drum
If your drum set doesn't include an isolated mounting system (see pages 60–61), mounting a well-tuned tom on its holder may drastically reduce its sustain, resonance, and tone. There are two solutions.

- You can fine-tune the drum **when mounted**. (Do mount the other rack tom well as both toms are bound to influence each other!)

123

- You can provide your toms with an **isolated mounting system**. These systems are not that expensive anymore.

- *Tip:* The first solution is not very musical, as you will find that the tom holder and/or the other rack tom now **dictates and usually severely limits the tuning range of the drum** — and that's not what a tom holder is meant to do.

Detuning

Drums detune because heads stretch quite a bit, especially when they're new. Detuning also occurs because the tension rods back up. Some drums come with a system to help prevent the latter (see page 48). Using softer, non-metal washers under the tension rods may help a bit, and will also make it easier to tune. Lug-locks are among the commercially available products that help prevent detuning by 'locking' the tension rods. As an alternative, get yourself a cake of violin rosin. Undo your tension rods and apply the rosin to the threaded part of the rods that goes into the lug nuts. This is a very affordable and effective way to keep them from backing up.

Press

Pressing a mounted, new head down with your hands helps taking the initial stretch out. If you do, you'll notice that it makes the pitch drop considerably. Some drummers even stand on their bass drum heads for this purpose. It can be done — but be careful.

The drum's pitch

You can also use the shell's pitch as a point of reference to

Actual notes

Some drummers tune their drums to actual notes: for example, the 10" to a G, the 12" to an E, and so on. Want to try this out? Then it's usually easiest to use a piano or a keyboard for reference pitches. Electronic tuners easily get confused when confronted with the many frequencies that drums produce. For drummers, the ears are a more reliable tool to gauge tuning.

124

determine the drum's optimum tuning range. First, take off all the drum's lugs and mounts. Then, put your arm inside the shell, and balance the shell on one finger. Now tap it lightly to determine its pitch, using a piano or another keyboard instrument, for example, for reference. Tune the drum to that fundamental pitch. This may help you get close to the point at which the drum sounds its best. You can also try this without taking all the hardware off: After all, that is how the drum will be used. As mounted hardware adds mass to the shell, this will definitely influence the pitch you hear.

Tuning devices

There are special devices that help you tune by measuring the resistance of each single tension rod or, more effectively, the tension of the head at each tension rod. The latter are not cheap, easily costing around seventy-five dollars or more, and fine-tuning is still up to you, but they can make basic tuning a lot faster. These devices also help you establish at which rod the tension is higher or lower — even when the pitches at various tension rods seem identical. The Tama Tension Watch was the first tuning aid of this kind.

Adjusting

Many drummers put the heads on with the logo in the same position (between the same two lugs) as the drum's badge. That way, if you take the head(s) off you'll always put them back in the same position — which helps tuning if the drum, the hoop or the head aren't perfectly round or level. They hardly ever are!

Thread

Tip: Some drum companies use tension rods that feature a finer thread (e.g. $10/32$" rather than $10/24$"), offering more control over the pitch when fine-tuning.

SNARE DRUM TUNING

Fine-tuning a snare drum is very similar to fine-tuning toms, the major difference being that both heads will be a lot tighter. If not, the sound will be more of a 'boosh', and less of a 'crack'.

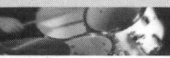

Ten lugs

Most snares have ten tension rods per head, making it hard to keep track of the tuning order. A tip: Write the numbers of the rods on the drum head, or on a ring cut from an old head.

Batter head

The batter head is typically tuned to a much higher tuning than the batter heads of the toms: After all, a 14" snare drum usually produces a higher pitch than the much smaller 10" tom in the same drum set.

Snare-side head

Likewise, the snare-side head needs to be much tighter than a tom's resonant head. Its main function is to make the snares respond properly: If you look at the snares while hitting the drum, you will see them bouncing off the snare-side head with each consecutive hit, which is what makes the snare drum sound like a snare drum. *Tip:* Mind your ears while doing this!

Feel

Because the snare-side head is so thin, it's hard to determine its exact pitch. A starting point to find the right tension is to put the tip of your left little finger against the top of your left thumb. Now feel how tight the fleshy part below your thumb is — and tune the snare side head so that it feels about the same.

Loose or tight

A relatively loose snare-side head will produce a 'loose', thick type

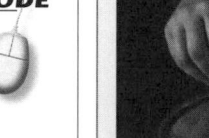

Tipcode Drum-018
Want to see how to make this bridge step by step? Then play this Tipcode!

of sound. Tightening it will increase clarity and projection, up to a point where it's so tight that the snares don't respond anymore.

Stick in a stick

If the snappy snares interfere with your snare head tuning, make them a bridge by separating them from the head. Simply — and very, very gently — insert a stick under the released snares, from left to right, the ends of the stick resting on the counter hoop, as shown below.

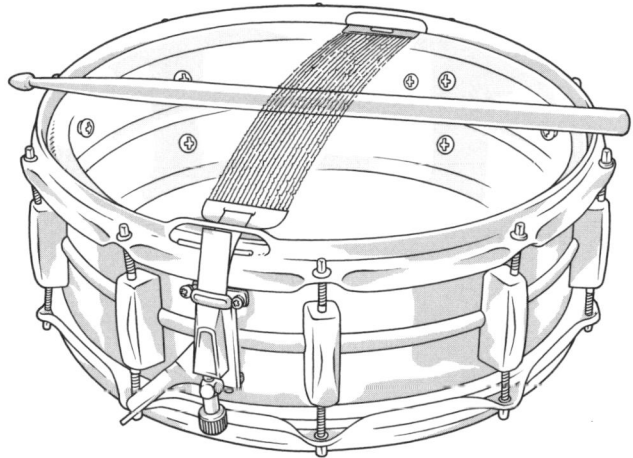

Make a 'bridge' for your snares.

The snares

Adjusting snare tension is best done in the 'on' position. If you need the drum to sound good at all volume levels, lightly tap the batter head while increasing the tension on the snares. As soon as they stop responding, the sound becoming kind of hollow, back up a little. If you play really loud, you can tighten the snares up a bit more.

Detuning the snare-side head

The snares are supposed to 'snap' when you strike the drum, and then be quiet right away. If they don't, one solution is to deliberately detune the snare-side head. Loosen the four tension rods at either end of the snares, and tighten the others a bit, to compensate. Now play the drum again, and note that it sounds as

127

if you have tightened the snares — so loosen them up a bit. When fine-tuning the snare-side head, the tension should now be highest at 1 and 2, a bit lower at rods 5, 8, 6 and 7, and lowest at the other four rods, as shown below.

Loosen these four tension rods a little and tighten up the rest to compensate.

loosen   loosen

The other way around

On some snare drums this trick only works if you do it the other way around: Tighten the rods at either end of the snares, and loosen the others. How much you'll have to change the tension depends on pretty much all the factors involved, so experiment.

Snare buzz

Snares are not supposed to respond when you play a tom or your bass drum, or when the rest of the band comes in — yet they do. Don't worry too much, as the resulting snare buzz is heard mainly by you, the drummer. However, if it gets too loud or distracting, there are a few things you can try.

128

• If your snares resonate when you play one of your toms, try

adapting the tuning of that tom. You can change its pitch, or try to keep the pitch the same by loosening the bottom and tightening the top head a little, or the other way around. No luck? Then you may have to change the tuning on your snare drum — or both.

• **Check the snares**. They're supposed to touch the snare-side head over their entire length. If you doubt their condition, take them off: They should rest flat on a tabletop. If not, replace them.

• The **distance between the snares and the drum's hoop** should be equal on both sides, and the strings or straps should pull evenly, right and left. Contrary to what you might expect, this is not the case on many new snare drums.

• The **snare strings** shouldn't be too thick. Shoelaces are. Your drum store sells special snare strings.

• One more option? If someone's playing a solo and you're not in, **release the snares.**

Different snares

The exact type of snares definitely influences your snare drum sound. There are snare sets with heavier and lighter strands; with strands made of harder or softer material; with less or more windings per inch; or with less of more strands. Their effect on the sound are kind of obvious.

The heavier the strands, the more strands and/or the more windings, the 'thicker' or heavier the snare drum will sound, while strands of a harder type of metal will make the sound a little brighter. Also, there are snare systems that feature non-spiral snare wires (similar to wound guitar strings) rather than the regular spiral snare wires.

Not on every drum

Not every set of snares will work with every snare drum. Obviously, an extra-wide set with thirty or even more strands makes no sense on a drum with a narrow snare bed.

129

BASS DRUM TUNING

Most drummers tune their bass drums really low, often to a point where the heads only just lose their wrinkles. You'll get more of a tone and less attack if you increase the tension, until the point where the drum starts choking again. Really high tunings are mainly used by jazz drummers, on small 18" bass drums.

Interval

As for the interval between the two heads and other tuning principles, bass drums generally behave like toms. Of course, a difference is that most bass drums are muffled, and many have cut-out front heads. A tip: The less muffling you use, the more important it is to apply even tension to both heads.

MUFFLING

For bass drums, tuning and muffling often go hand in hand. Many drummers muffle their snare drums too. Toms are generally allowed to sound wide open.

Muffling the bass drum

There are many ways to reduce the bass drum's tone and ring. Here are some examples.

- First, there's a wide variety of **commercially available muffling systems** for bass drums. Visit your dealer and talk to other drummers!

- For light muffling, check out bass drum heads with **built-in muffling rings** (see page 89).

- A very affordable and effective alternative is to use the **traditional felt strip**, at about one third of the way along the head(s). The strip bounces off the head at the attack, just like a muffling ring. Felt strips can also be used on the front head

only, combined with a heavier type of muffling of the batter head, for example. *Tip:* You can easily lower the strip's tension by stretching it as bit: Simply pull it away from the head. To make it sit tighter, you need to remove the head.

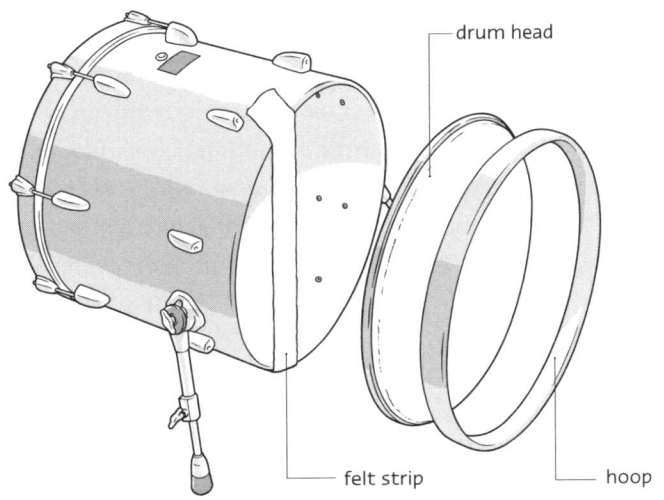

drum head

felt strip   hoop

Bass drum with felt strip.

- You can buy **special bass drum pillows** that bounce off the head at the moment of impact, allowing for a full-sized attack sound and muffling what comes later.

- **A rolled-up towel**, taped in the angle where head(s) and shell meet, is a lot cheaper. It sounds different too, as it stays in contact with the head.

- Another old-fashioned, effective, cheap (but not easily adjustable) way to muffle the bass drum is to partially fill it with **shredded newspaper**, or small pieces of polystyrene.

- For a really short sound, try putting a sheet of 1" or 2" **polystyrene** or foam plastic around the inside of the shell, barely touching the head(s) — or simply put a pillow or a blanket inside the drum.

- If your bass drum sound has too much ring or tone to it, you can **detune one or both heads**. It's fast, effective and very low-budget, and it's also great if you need a tighter sound for just one or two songs.

Felt strip tips

If you want to use a felt strip for muffling, first remove the head. Place the felt strip over the drum, locating its ends at two of the drum's lugs. This allows you to tuck these loose ends under the tension rods. Alternatively, you can place the head over the felt strip; then place the hoop over the head and stick one or both ends of the strip between the head and the hoop. The exact location of the strip affects the amount of muffling, of course. The more you move it to the middle, the more it will affect the sound. For starters, put it at about $1/3$ of the drum (see the illustration on the previous page).

The front head

For a long time, bass drums were played without the resonant front head, effectively reducing resonance as well as sustain. A less drastic solution is to cut a hole in the front head, or buy a pre-cut (*ported*) front head. If the hole is in the middle of the head, directly opposite the beater, the effect will soon be similar to having no head at all, even if it's just a small hole: The sound will fly straight out, so to speak.

Smaller hole

By contrast, a small (4"–6") hole at a couple of inches from the edge will hardly affect the sound at all. Holes like this are often made so that a microphone can be stuck inside the drum, and they also give access to the inside of the instrument, for instance so that you can adjust its internal muffling. The general rule: the larger the hole, the more attack and the less tone and resonance. A hole also reduces the rebound of the batter head: the larger the hole, the less rebound.

The entire head

Removing the entire head may result in rattling lug nuts, a deformed bass drum shell, and damaged bearing edges (and lost tension rods). It's better to cut out most of the head, leaving just two or three inches around the perimeter.

132

The template and the edge

Many drummers use a cymbal as a template when cutting a hole. However, should your hand slip when you're holding the knife, you'll do less damage if you use a lid or any other flat metal disc instead. There are special templates too, as well as products to cover the sharp edge of the hole. A household alternative is to cut a piece of thin rubber tubing (*i.e.*, gasoline tubing) open lengthwise, and mount it over the edge. Cutting drum heads requires a sharp knife, so make sure to cut nothing but the drum head and be very careful!

Attack

Increasing the attack sound of a bass drum can also be done by using a hard (wood or plastic) beater, or by sticking a special self-adhesive pad on the point of attack. These pads are made by various drum head and other companies. A cheap alternative: Use duct tape to stick a relatively large coin to the head at the point of impact. As hard beaters are more likely to dent the bass drum head, they are often used in combination with bass drum pads — which increases the attack even further.

MUFFLING SNARES AND TOMS

There are various ways to muffle snare drums and toms. Some work for both, others for snare drums only.

O-ring

The O-ring that comes with many snare drums is very effective. These rings mute the entire circumference of the head, which is where most (both desirable and undesirable) overtones are generated. You can also buy these rings separately, or carefully cut them yourself, using an old head. The wider the ring, the more marked the effect will be. A head with a built-in O-ring or muffling ring (see page 89) will generally help produce a more open type of sound, compared to using an O-ring on top of the head. O-rings are rarely used on toms; they muffle the sound too

much, they strongly reduce the drum's sustain, and they may buzz as tom heads move a lot more than the (much tighter!) snare drum head.

An O-ring down-under

If you like the O-ring to stay put at your snare drum, you can take an old 14" head and cut the middle 12 to 13 inches out of the head. Then cut the flesh hoop off. Take the batter head off the drum you want to muffle, place the remaining drum head ring over the bearing edge, put the batter head back on, and tune the drum.

Tape

Duct tape (also known as *stage tape, gaffer tape, cloth tape* or *duck tape*) works well on snare drums and toms. It's inexpensive, easy to apply and remove, and very 'experimentable'. Locate the best spot by gently putting your finger on various places on the head while playing the drum at the same time. Folding the tape into fins increases the muffling. For a really dry sound, you can tape a paper tissue to the head.

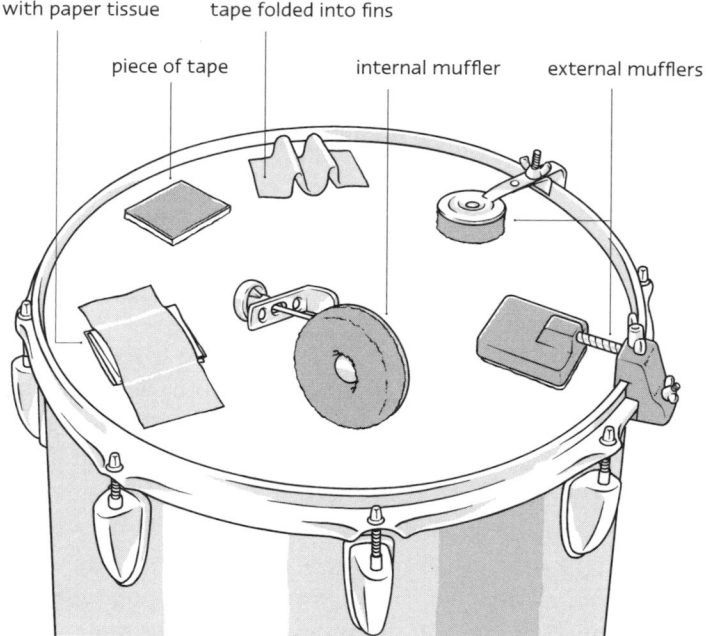

tape with paper tissue   tape folded into fins

piece of tape   internal muffler   external mufflers

Gel

As an alternative for tape, you may use commercially available gel damper pads. These sticky pads are re-usable, they can be cut to size for minimal damping, and they're very effective on all types of drums — and even on cymbals.

The outer edge

The outer edge of the drum head produces much of the high, crisp overtones that make rim shots and rim clicks speak. O-rings muffle that area — so you may have better results with mufflers (or pieces of tape, or gel pads) that muffle the head in a smaller area only.

Internal and external mufflers

Mufflers can be divided in *internal* and *external* mufflers.

- Internal mufflers restrict the downward movement of the head, which is very noticeable on toms — so they're hardly used on those drums anymore. As this type of muffler leaves the head entirely open, many brush players still like it on snare drums.

- External mufflers are flexible, and they're fast and easy to work with. They're rare, though. One reason is that they don't move along with the head as easily as tape does, for example. They also take up (be it a little) space in the playing area, and you usually have to take them off for transportation.

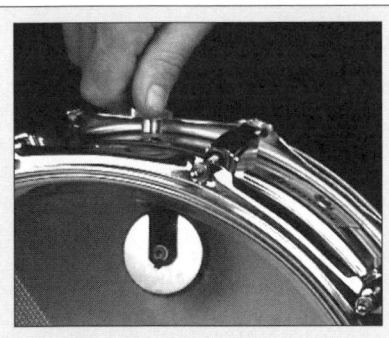

Tipcode Drum-019
Adjusting an old-fashioned but still very effective internal muffler is shown in this Tipcode.

 **TIPCODE**

Tune, tune, tune

Snare drums and toms are often muffled to reduce the effect of

135

unwanted, clashing overtones — but these are actually the result of badly tuned heads. The better you tune a drum, the less you have to muffle it. More importantly, the more you muffle a drum, the less you'll be able to hear what you paid for!

Miking

If your set is about to be miked, spend extra time tuning it, as microphones easily pick up unwanted overtones. A properly tuned set with an isolated mounting system for the toms is less likely to get its heads covered in tape by a sound engineer who otherwise can't handle the sound of your drums.

Muffling and volume

The only way to muffle your drums so that your neighbors can get some rest is to stuff them with polystyrene, or cover them with rubber discs (see page 22). The types of muffling discussed in this chapter barely reduce the number of decibels you produce.

11

Setting up and maintenance

Drummers are among the only musicians who can tailor their instruments to fit them like a glove. This chapter offers some basic tips, and also deals with keeping everything in working order and taking your drums on the road.

If you want to save energy and gain speed and control, the best way to set up your drums is so that you can reach every piece of your instrument without really stretching your arms at any time. The drums in the illustration on page 7 have been set up that way.

The throne

As a starting point, adjust the height of your throne so that your thighs are parallel to the floor. If you're young — and small — this can make it hard to reach your toms and cymbals. Buying a smaller set (see page 19) helps. A no-budget alternative is to remove the second rack tom, so you can lower your most important cymbal, the ride.

The pedals

Position the pedals so that your shins are angled slightly forwards. Set the length of the spurs of the bass drum so that the bottom of the front hoop is raised one or two inches off the floor. The bass drum beater should hit the head close to the middle of the drum.

The snare drum

Position your snare drum so that the batter head is one or two inches higher than your thigh. If you use *matched grip* (the same grip for both hands), tilt the drum towards you slightly. Drummers who play *traditional grip* often tilt it towards the floor tom.

The toms

Set the floor tom at the same height as (the lower side of) the snare drum, and consider angling it slightly towards it. The rack toms should be angled towards you, again slightly. If the angle is too steep, you'll end up with dented heads: The larger the angle between stick and head, the more easily you'll dent the head. Position the toms so that the lower sides of the batter heads are about four to eight inches higher than your snare and floor tom heads. When set right, they're not so high that you would need to raise your arms to play your rack toms, and not so low that you can't play rim shots on them.

The cymbals

Angle the cymbals towards you as well, to make them easier to

138

play and harder to crack. Have the hi-hats about four inches higher then the snare drum, slightly overlapping it, as a starting point. The distance between the two cymbals determines how far your foot has to travel. Loud players often have their hi-hats higher and further apart, and vice versa.

CYMBAL TIPS

If you're a heavy drummer and if you use heavy sticks, you should use pretty heavy cymbals, or you're bound to use a lot of cymbals — one after the other. Yet some heavy drummers play pretty thin crashes without ever breaking them. How come? They have good

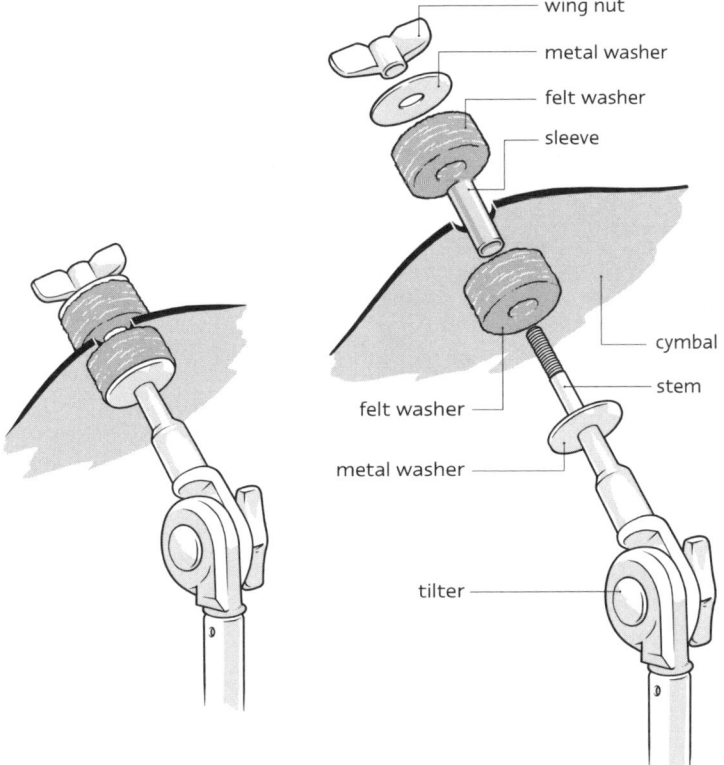

Cymbal tilter.

wing nut
metal washer
felt washer
sleeve

cymbal
stem
felt washer
metal washer

tilter

139

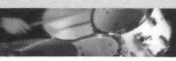

playing technique, for one thing, and they don't try to play *through* the cymbal. Here are a few more tips.

* The stem of the cymbal tilter should always be covered with a **nylon sleeve**, or, as one of many alternatives, a piece of rubber tubing such as gasoline tubing. Without it, you'll create a keyhole in the cymbal, and it may crack from the hole. Also, the cymbal should rest on a **felt, leather or synthetic washer**.

* Never tighten cymbals down. Crashes and splashes especially should be allowed a generous amount of give, so they can **go with the blow.** Replacing the traditional retainer nuts with alternative products (see page 80) helps prevent over-tightening cymbals.

* The clutch should be set so that the top cymbal has a little **bit of play** too. First turn the bottom nut to where it stops. Then adjust the first upper nut for the desired amount of play, and fix it in place with the second upper nut (the upper upper one, that is).

TIPCODE

Tipcode Drum-020 and 021
These Tipcodes show you how to mount your top cymbal and how to adjust and lock its desired amount of play.

Stop

A piece of carpet is all you need to keep your bass drum and hi-hat from creeping. Use short-pile carpet. The softer the carpet is, the more it'll muffle your sound. The minimum size is dictated by the surface you need for your throne, your bass drum, your hi-hat, and any extra pedals. Did you leave home without a carpet? Then use a piece of rope to tie your pedals to your throne. Want to save time setting up? Use tape (removable) or paint (non-removable) to

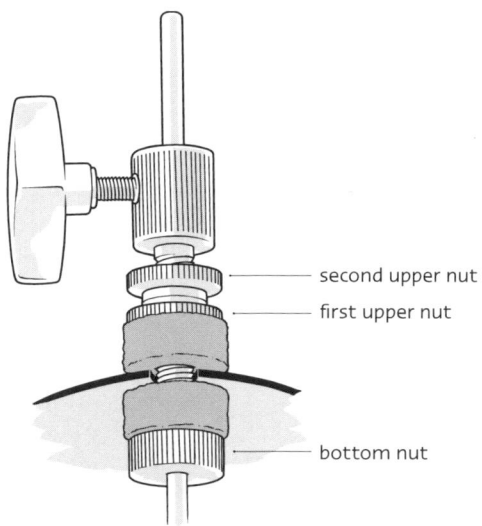

second upper nut

first upper nut

bottom nut

mark the positions of stands, pedals, and drums on the carpet.
A professional alternative for carpets and tape is offered by
Drumplates.

Left or right?

If you happen to be left-handed, you can go for a variety of
solutions.

- You can **mirror the entire setup** as shown on the next page
  This may be awkward if you share the instrument with
  others, though, and it makes it harder to sit in: Most sets are
  configured for right-handed drummers.

- As an alternative, just **move the ride cymbal** to the left side
  of the set. Some right-handed drummers do that too, having
  trained themselves to keep time with their (initially slower)
  left hand. Why? Because this way they don't have to cross their
  arms anymore, as all right-handed drummers have to when
  keeping time with their right hand on the hi-hat — which is on
  their left side.

- Teach yourself to play a regular '**right-handed**' set. After
  all, left-handed pianists and sax players (to name just two
  examples) play regular 'right-handed' instruments too…

141

... mirror the entire setup...

MAINTENANCE AND CLEANING

Keeping your drum set in good working order is largely a matter of checking its nuts and bolts from time to time. When changing heads, check the bolts that keep the lugs in place. Never over-tighten them, as that'll restrict the vibrations of the shell. Loose-fitting parts may start buzzing and rattling. Are you about to record your drums? Then carefully double-check your entire set for any unwanted sounds: Studio microphones tend to hear things you never did. Be prepared to come across rattles and other noise that seems to originate from nowhere.

Oil
A few tiny drops of oil once in a while make your pedals move more smoothly. Stiff or jerky tension rods can be cured the same way, unless you're dealing with jagged washers (often overlooked), tension rods, or lug nuts.

More checks

Have a look at the snare strings or straps, and replace them when they show signs of wearing out. The same goes for the sleeves on your cymbal stands. Have a look at your pedals too, and check if everything is as tight or as loose as it's supposed to be. Also check for play in parts that are not supposed to move, and consult your dealer if you find any.

Cleaning

A soft cloth is all you need to keep your instrument shiny, if you use it frequently. Glass cleaners work fine on covered drums. There are special cleaners for drums with lacquered, stained, waxed, or oiled shells. Check with your dealer! Regular furniture cleaners may leave a greasy residue on your shells.

Cymbals

Use chrome polish for chrome-plated parts only, and never on cymbals. If you want to be on the safe side, use genuine cymbal cleaners only, following the instructions on the packaging closely. Some cymbal cleaners are more abrasive than others. A few brands offer special cleaners for B20 or B8 bronze, the latter being less abrasive. Household detergents and water are good for cleaning cymbals, but don't make them shine. Always rinse and dry your cymbals thoroughly when you've finished cleaning. *Tip:* Many cymbals have a very thin protective coating or finish that keeps them looking like new for a while. Using a cleaner will remove this finish.

ON THE ROAD

Here are some important tips for when you take your set on the road.

- Treat your instruments to a set of **gig bags or cases**, preferably the ones that have some kind of shock-absorbing lining. Bags, which usually have shoulder straps, are easier to carry than most cases. Gig bags and fiber cases are not always waterproof.

Plastic cases are, but they're heavier and often cost more. Hard-shell **flight cases** are very good, very heavy and quite expensive.

Two cases and a gig bag.

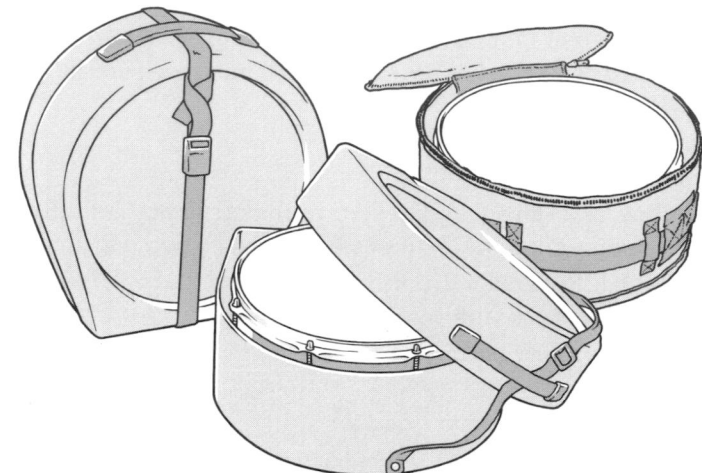

- **Your cymbals** need to be packed too, more than any other part of your set. For one thing, the edges are very vulnerable. Some bags offer extra protection in that area. Cases usually have a center bolt, which keeps the edges from being damaged.

- Cymbal bags usually come with **separators**, which keep your cymbals from scratching each other. A shoulder strap is almost a must.

A cymbal bag with separators between the cymbals, handles, and an adjustable shoulder strap.

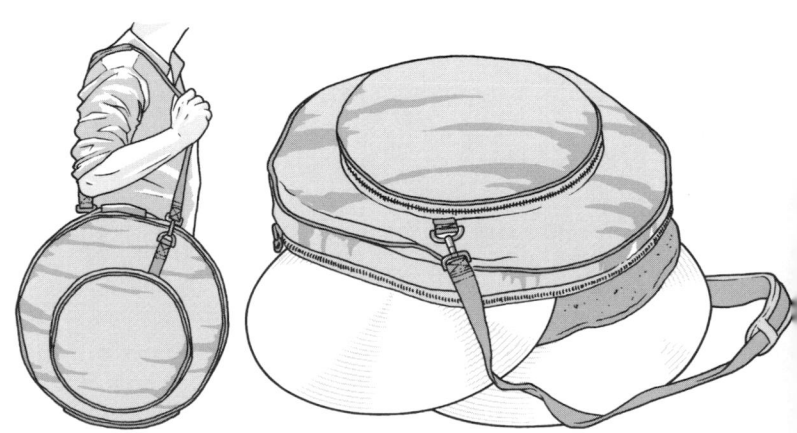

144

- Always have **spare heads** with you, at least for your two most important drums: the snare drum (batter and snare-side head!) and the bass drum (batter). Simply keep these heads in the corresponding drum cases or bags, or in your car (with your spare tire, for instance).

- Put some **extra sticks and brushes** in you car, just in case you happen to arrive at a gig without your stick bag.

- Brushes don't break, but they can **let go of their wires** all of a sudden — so bring a spare set.

- **Other items to bring**: snare strings or straps, a pair of pliers, a screwdriver, duct tape (for muffling, eliminating rattles, and emergency repairs), cymbal sleeves, washers, tension rods, felt washers, and a spare clutch (check to see if it fits your pull rod; they come in different sizes). If possible, also bring a spare bass drum pedal.

- Want to **set up fast**? Use hose clamps on hardware items that don't come with memory locks.

- If you play amplified most of the time, you might consider buying your **own microphones**. There are special drummer's mics that attach to the hoops, and systems to attach mics inside the shells. Microphone prices have gone down!

- If drums have **serial numbers**, you'll usually find them on the badge. Jot them down (see pages 226–227). Cymbals may have a serial number, too.

- Consider **insuring your instrument**, especially if you take it on the road. Musical instruments fall under the insurance category of 'valuables'. A regular homeowner insurance policy will not cover all possible damage, whether it occurs at home, on the road, in the studio or onstage.

- Never leave your instruments **unattended in a car**.

12

Back in time

The human voice is undoubtedly the oldest instrument around. Drums come second. The drum set, however, is a recent addition to the world of musical instruments. And cymbals? They go back hundreds of years.

It didn't take mankind very long to find out that hitting things sounds good, and hitting hollow things sounds even better. Hollow tree trunks, for instance. Presumably, the drum was born on the day that someone stretched an animal skin over the top of a hollow tree trunk and struck it. Since that day, hundreds of drums and percussion instruments have been invented.

Two drummers

The very first jazz bands had two drummers. One played the snare drum. The second played the bass drum with one hand and the predecessor of the hi-hat with the other: The bottom cymbal, mounted on top of the drum, was played by simply hitting it with the top cymbal.

The pedals

Around 1909, William F. Ludwig came up with the first modern bass drum pedal, which allowed one drummer to play bass and snare drums simultaneously. An extra rod was attached to it,

Carlton Ridgmount Console (1935). Note the rack (on wheels!), the cowbells, the temple blocks, and the T-rods for the batter heads of the toms. The toms have non-tunable, tacked on bottom heads. Collection of the Classic Drum Museum, England.

hitting a small cymbal as you played the bass drum. This primitive attachment eventually made way for the low-hat, a lower version of today's hi-hat. It took another twenty-odd years (!) for someone to come up with the idea to lengthen the tube, raising the cymbals to a height where they could be played with sticks as well.

Toms
The early drummers used so-called Chinese toms, which had tacked-on heads. Tunable toms were introduced some time in the mid-1930s, and drum sets haven't changed all that much since then.

Heads
One of the few major changes in the history of the drum set came in the late 1950s when plastic drum heads slowly started to replace the traditional calf skin heads. Calf skin sounds great, but plastic heads are more consistent and reliable, and plastic is not sensitive to changes in humidity. Calf skin heads, by contrast, need to be retuned the moment somebody in a wet coat enters the club you're playing in.

Twenty sizes
The first cymbals were very thick and heavy, and were used in all kinds of rituals and processions, and in military music. The modern cymbal was born in Turkey in 1623, credited to Avedis Zildjian I. Terms such as ride, crash and splash are of a much later date. A 1948 catalog, for instance, simply mentions twenty different sizes (from 7" to 26") in six different weights, from Paper Thin to Heavy.

TIPBOOK DRUMS

13

The percussion family

The word percussion comes from the Latin word for hitting, 'percussio.' Every instrument that you play by hitting it is part of this large family, with thousands and thousand of family members. The following chapter covers no more than a few popular examples.

When drummers talk about percussionists, they usually refer to *Latin percussionists*, playing any combination of instruments such as congas, bongos, timbales, cowbells, shakers, rattles, scrapers — and more. The main hand drums are the tall congas and the much shallower, high-pitched bongos. Bongos are always played in pairs. Congueros often use two congas, and sometimes three or more. Most congas and bongos still come with animal skin heads, but plastic heads are gaining acceptance.

Timbales

Timbales are typical Latin-American drums. They usually come with metal shells that are quite similar to metal snare drum shells. Their single plastic heads are typically played with special timbale sticks (no tip, no taper!), which are also used to play the shells (*cascara*). Most timbaleros also mount one or more cowbells and a cymbal on their stand.

cowbells

congas

timbales

Symphonic and concert drums

In symphony orchestras and concert bands, there's often a separate musician for every percussion instrument. The *tympani*,

for instance, with big, spherical copper shells and single heads that are tuned to specific pitches. *Concert bass drums* measure up to 40" and more. Cymbals are often played in pairs. If they're stand mounted, they're referred to as *suspended cymbals*.

Marching bands

Marching drummers use so called *field drums*. Their snare drums are very deep, and typically tuned extremely high. In marching bands, single-headed *timp-toms* (also known as *tenor drums* or *multi-tenors*) take the place of the drummer's toms. They're mounted on a harness, just like the bass drums. Marching bass drums have a relatively shallow shell, and they're available in various diameters.

Electronic drumming

Electronic drums have more and more to offer each year, in sound, playability, and features. Many sets have tunable heads that feel like 'real' drums; others use rubber pads that feel and look

An electronic drum set (Roland).

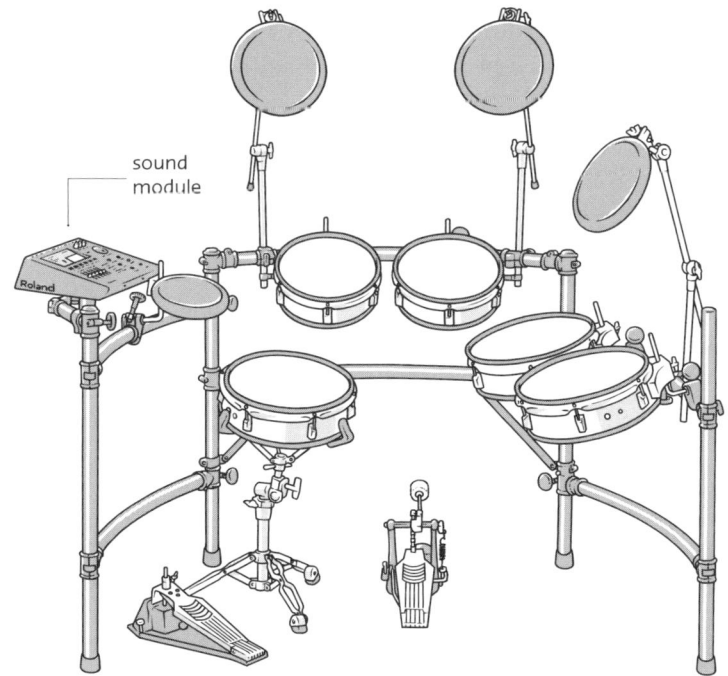

sound module

153

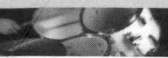

much like practice pads. What you play is picked up by the pads' built-in triggers that activate digitally recorded sounds (*samples*), stored in the *sound module*. These modules offer a large number of percussive and other sounds, as well as pre-programmed drum kits. Sounds and kits can be edited to your liking. Other common features include a built-in metronome and play-along sequences. More expensive sets have higher quality sounds, higher numbers of sounds and preset kits, extended editing and mixing facilities, more inputs, and other features. Electronic drums are great for silent practicing, and they're popular in studios as well.

Digital interface
Like most other electronic instruments, electronic drums can be hooked up to digital recording gear, your computer, and other digital equipment through *MIDI* (Musical Instrument Digital Interface), offering unlimited options.

Acoustic, yet digital
Samples can also be activated from your acoustic drum set, either by using triggers on your regular drums, or by using additional pads. Some companies produce special small *trigger pads*, designed to be added to your drum set.

Drum machines
Most drummers feel that drum machines are operated, rather than played. They can be used to practice with (they're more fun than a metronome), and in studio situations.

Mallet instruments
Melodic percussion instruments have metal or wooden keys arranged in a way similar to a piano keyboard. The fact that they're played with mallets explains their other name, *mallet instruments*.

• A *glockenspiel* has a series of small metal keys, producing a piercing, bell-like sound. Orchestral glockenspiels are also known as *orchestral bells*.

• *Xylophones*, used in both marching and orchestral settings, have narrow wooden or plastic keys with small resonators.

154

- A *marimba* has wider, larger wooden keys with large resonators, making for a much warmer tone.

- *Vibraphones* are mainly used in jazz bands. Its wide metal keys have resonators with rotating metal discs that make the instrument's sound vibrate.

Different drums

Hundreds of cultures have their own drums, bells, gongs, and other ethnic percussion instruments. Some of them have been adapted to the demands of Western percussionists. The *djembe*, for instance, is a very popular African, rope-tensioned drum. Western variations have a tuning system that you also find on congas, a similarly built wood or fiberglass shell, and often a plastic head.

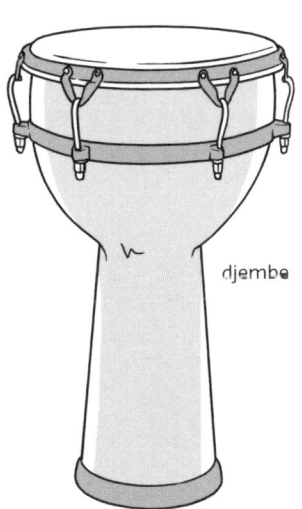

djembe

Another African drum that has been adapted is the *talking drum*. You hold this drum under your upper arm and by clenching your arm you tighten the ropes that connect the two heads. The resulting pitch differences are a language of their own. Some other examples of popular instruments are Brazilian drums ranging from the low *surdo* to the high-pitched *repinique*, the Latin American *cajon* (a wooden case that you both sit and play on), and all kinds of single-headed frame drums, which look like big tambourines without jingles.

Big drums

Traditional Japanese drummers use sticks as thick as your wrist. The biggest Japanese drum, the *odaiko*, is cut out of an enormous tree and weighs close to five hundred pounds. The world's biggest bass drum was much lighter: Built in 1997 by the Dutch company Vancore, this drum featured 165" heads.

155

14

How they're made

There are many different ways to make drums, cymbals, heads, and sticks: completely by hand, using computer-controlled machines, or anything in between. This chapter gives you a basic idea of the various manufacturing processes.

One of the main things you need to make a regular plywood drum is a mold — which easily costs as much as a decent car. Most drums are made up of wooden sheets that consist of three plies each, the grains running in alternating directions (cross laminating). These sheets are cut to very exact sizes, glued, and then pressed around the inside of the mold. The drying process is usually sped up using heat or microwave technology. When the shells come out, they are cut to length and the bearing edges are cut and sanded.

TIPCODE

Tipcode Drum-022
A brief visit to a drum factory, showing how drums are made, finished, and assembled.

Folding the wood around the inside of the mold.

158

The finish
Lacquered drums wear many coats: stain, color, and one or more clear, protective coats. Shells are sanded or polished after every coat. The cover on covered drums is applied using glue or double-sided adhesive tape. After the shell has been drilled, the drum can be assembled. Not all drum manufacturers produce their own shells, and most do not make their own lugs, hoops, and other metal parts.

CYMBALS

Cymbals basically start out as flat, round discs. For their B20 cymbals (see page 106), most companies cast their own bronze, producing thick, round castings, one for each cymbal. These castings are then rolled down to flat discs in multiple steps. For most other cymbals the flat discs are made elsewhere. Italian cymbal makers have always used molds that already have the basic shape of a cymbal.

Tipcode Drum-023
This film shows the traditional way of making hand-hammered cymbals.

TIPCODE

The shape
Traditionally, cymbals are shaped using hammers. Only few, mostly smaller companies still do this entirely by hand. Most manufacturers use either mechanical hammers (rotating the cymbal under the hammer by hand), automatic hammers, or computer-controlled hammers. The latter are even used for 'hand-hammered' cymbals in some cases. Sometimes, the cymbals are

159

given an initial shape by pressing them before hammering. The cup is nearly always made by a press.

The ancient art of hand-hammering.

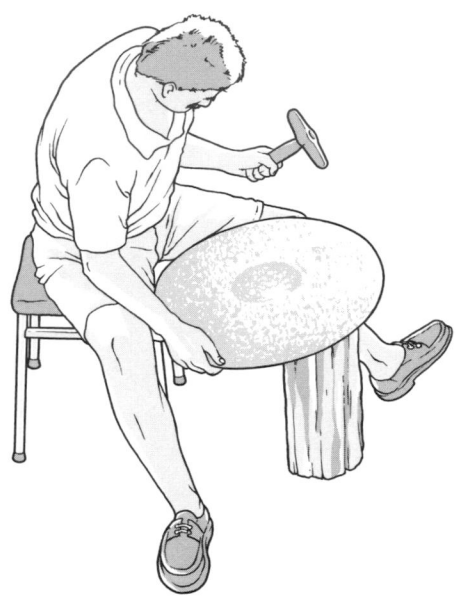

Spinforming

Many less expensive cymbals are spinformed: They are forced in shape against a rotating die. These cymbals are often recognizable by a wide, continuous, even groove on one side. In the late 1990s, some companies started using this technique on B20 cymbals too.

Lathing

The fine grooves that you see on many cymbals are created on a lathe, the worker (or a machine) moving a hardened steel knife over the surface of the rotating cymbal. This process makes the cymbals shine and it opens up the sound. Unlathed cymbals have a 'tighter' sound, generally speaking. A buffing process may be involved as a final step.

Finish

Most cymbals are finished with an ultra-thin coating, making them less susceptible to fingerprints and other stains. The coating is generally said not to influence the sound, and it disappears over the years — or even sooner if you use a cymbal cleaner.

STICKS

Wooden sticks start out as timber that has been cured and cut down to square dowels about one inch across. A grindstone, or a knife with a blade in the shape of a stick, removes exactly the right amount of wood along the length of the rotating dowel. One way of finishing the sticks is to put hundreds of them in a big barrel and throw in some lacquer or wax. Then spin the barrel for a while, and you're done.

HEADS

Basically, there are two ways of making drum heads. Remo, Evans, and Aquarian use a kind of resin to 'glue' the heads inside the flesh hoop. Other companies fold the head around a square rod inside the flesh hoop before clamping it down. In all cases, the heads are cut out of large sheets of film, with the collar being formed using heated presses.

15

Brands

In this chapter you'll meet some of the main drum and cymbal brands, and a few smaller ones too. Some of the drum brands sell in all price ranges, others concentrate either on the lower or the higher end of the market. The few large cymbal companies offer an extensive range of instruments as well. Most smaller ones sell higher-budget cymbals only.

There are ten major brands offering a variety of drum series in pretty much every price range, from low-budget to high-end instruments.

> ### Time sensitive
> Note that the information in this chapter is more time-sensitive than the contents of any of the other chapters in this book: New brands are introduced from time to time, others are re-introduced or discontinued; factories are closed, brand names are sold — and so on.

For many years Drum Workshop concentrated on the high-end market with both pedals and drums. With the introduction of the Pacific division in 2000 (PDP), the products of the company became available in lower price ranges too.

ℓUDWIG®

The American Ludwig company introduced the first modern bass drum pedal in 1909. Other legendary designs are the Supra-phonic snare drum and the Speed King bass drum pedal.

MAPEX®

Mapex came on the scene in the early 1990s. The company had been making parts and drums for other brands for many years prior to introducing their own drums under the Mapex name.

One of Pearl's claims to fame is the Pearl Export, the world's best-selling drum set ever. In 1995, the one millionth set was made. Pearl built their first drums in Japan in 1950. Their basic tom holder and bass drum spur designs have been widely copied.

Premier

Premier (UK) has been around since 1922. Numerous classic Premier innovations, from double lugs to convertible boom stands and collapsible lugs, were introduced subsequently as novelties by other companies.

REMO® USA

Drummer Remo Belli was one of the pioneers of the plastic drum head in 1957. The American Remo company later introduced the wood-resin based Acousticon as the shell material for its own drums. Acousticon is also used for percussion instruments.

♪ SONOR®

Sonor (Germany, 1875), the oldest company in this list, has long been known for making pretty much every part in-house, and for its use of slotted tension rods. The company introduced their first Asian-made low-budget sets in 2000.

TAMA®

Tama's original brand name, Star, is still part of the names of all their series. Tama has always played a major role in hardware

developments, such as the boom stand, the multi-clamp, and the 'basket-less' Air Ride snare stand.

The first Taye drum sets were made in 1999, based on 25 years of experience of making drums and parts for other companies. Ray Ayotte, founder of the Canadian company of that name, is the company's president.

Yamaha is one of the largest companies in the music industry, producing a large number of other instruments as well as drums, not to mention motor cycles, hi-fi systems, sailboats, and other products. Few modern sets have been on the market as long as their Recording Custom series, introduced in 1975.

Elsewhere

Most of the companies above also have instruments or parts made in other countries; Taiwan, China, Korea, or Indonesia, for instance — but also in Europe.

US drum companies

Gretsch and **Slingerland** are two of the older US companies. Their first instruments date back to 1883 and 1921, respectively. **Rogers**, another brand with a long history, built its last US sets in 1983.

More names

Other, younger companies that produce drums in various price ranges include **ddrum**, originally known for their digital drums, and **Cadeson**, from Taiwan.

166

BUDGET PRICE RANGE AND UP

Many brands only or mainly offer drum sets in the low and medium budget price ranges. Some of these brand names belong to Asian companies, others are owned by American companies that have their instruments made in Asian countries such as China, Taiwan, and Korea. A few better-known examples are **Basix**, **CB Percussion**, **Cannon Percussion**, **Coda**, **Dixon**, **Peace**, **Rockwood**, **Stagg**, **Sunlite**, and **WorldMax**. Some of these companies offer a wider range of instruments and feature more original designs than others.

Your own brand

As with any other type of instrument, more or less anyone can have his own brand of drums made. As long as the order is big enough, you can simply pick a shell design, select the lugs, hoops, holders, and spurs, have a logo and a badge designed, and a new brand is born — often offering good value for money, as little is spent on research and development, or on endorsements.

HIGH-END AND MORE

If you want the best gear money can buy, you can either look at the high-end series of the brands listed earlier, or at one of the companies that concentrate on high-end instruments only. What does 'high-end' mean? Well, consider buying a single bass drum for the price of three or four low-budget five-piece drum sets...

Shells and hardware

Hardly any of the high-end companies make their own shells, nor their own hardware. Their main activities are design, research, and development, besides assembling and finishing the drums. More often than not, the shells will be supplied by Keller, a US furniture company that offers shells in pretty much any configuration. Another name you may come across is Jasper.

167

High-end US

Some of the main high-end US brand names are **Craviotto**, **Dunnett**, **GMS**, **Grover**, **Innovation Drum**, **Lang**, **Noble & Cooley**, **Pork Pie Percussion**, and **Spaun**. A complete listing of US drum brands would include dozens of names.

Other countries

The number of high-end and other, smaller drum companies in other countries is considerably smaller, but they certainly do exist. One of the better known high-end drum makers is Ayotte, from Canada. Another Canadian brand is Luka Percussion. England has **Noonan**, Greece has **Gabriel**, and France has **Capelle**. **Brady** and **Sleishman** are made in Australia, and **RMV** and **Odery** come from Brazil. In Italy, **Le Soprano** and **Tamburo** produce stave drums. Similar drums are made in Belgium under the name of **Lignum**. German companies include **Handschuh Solid Drums**, **Troyan**, and **Wahan**. Not all of these drums are available worldwide.

Lower prices

Some of the companies listed above feature lower priced drums as well, *e.g.*, drums with non-US shells and series with drums in a limited number of sizes and colors, rather than custom instruments.

Different shell materials

Various companies build drums with non-wood shells. The early 2000s showed a return of acrylic (see-through) drums, for example. Other materials include fiberglass (used by **Impact** and **Tempus**, for example), carbon fiber (**Rocket** and, again, **Tempus**), and aluminum. **Traps** makes very portable shell-less kits.

Hardware

Some companies produce hardware only, including **Gibraltar**, **Axis** (best known for their bass drum pedals), and **Rock-N-Soc** (thrones).

CYMBAL BRANDS

As basic as a cymbal looks, making one is not at all easy — and that's just one of the reasons why the number of factories producing them is very small.

The Turkish city of Istanbul is where the modern cymbal was born, nearly four centuries ago. The Istanbul company was founded in the early 1980s. Twenty years later, the number of cymbal factories in the city had risen to six: Anatolian, Bosphorus, Istanbul Agop, Istanbul Mehmet, and Turkish Cymbals. In later years, even more companies introduced handmade Turkish cymbals, including Agean, Amedia, Masterwork, and TRX. Alchemy cymbals are made by Istanbul Agop.

MEINL

The German Meinl company started in 1953. For many years, the company concentrated on the lower end of the market. In the late 1990s, Meinl's professional ranges started growing, and the company largely expanded its range of percussion instruments.

PAISTE

The Swiss cymbal makers at Paiste made their name with the classic 2002 series, which is still around. In the late 1980s they introduced the Paiste Sound Alloy, a new alloy for professional cymbals. Paiste has always been widely represented in all price ranges.

169

Sabian (Canada) made their debut with two series of professional cymbals in 1981, gradually expanding the number of series ever since, in all price-ranges. Sabian is one of the few factories to make signature cymbals, which are developed in co-operation with well-known drummers.

A merger of a number of small Italian cymbal makers led to the establishment of UFIP in 1931. There's still a lot of handwork involved in their professional series, which were thoroughly revised in the 1990s.

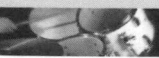

The Zildjian company dates back to 1623, when the Armenian Avedis Zildjian discovered how to treat bronze in such a way that you could make great cymbals out of it. Even after almost four centuries, the current president is still a direct descendant of Avedis Zildjian.

MORE CYMBALS

Some other cymbal brands:

- **Orion**, from Brazil, is a relatively young cymbal company, having started in 1999. Orion makes cymbals in all price ranges.

- **Saluda** (South Carolina, 1997) buys cymbal blanks in China and hammers, lathes and finishes them in the US.

- As with drums and most other instruments, there are more cymbal brands than there are manufacturers. **Camber**, for example, was a cymbal brand made by Sabian until 2006. Likewise, some of the Turkish cymbal makers produce cymbals for other companies.

- Low-budget Asian drum sets often come with Asian cymbals that either carry no name, or the brand name of the drums.

China

Most Chinese cymbals come from the province of Wuhan, where cymbals are still made the way they were decades ago. Chinese cymbal makers don't limit themselves to Chinese cymbals: They make 'Turkish' cymbals as well. Brand names include **Wuhan**, **Stagg**, and **Dream**.

171

TIPBOOK DRUMS

16

Setups

A drum set can be as big or as small as you like — from just a bass drum, a snare drum, a hi-hat, and a single cymbal to setups with three or more bass drums, and anything in between. The four examples in this chapter are just that: examples. After all, the definitive rock drum set is just as imaginary as the definitive rock drummer.

BASIC, STANDARD FIVE-PIECE SETUP

Most drummers start on this basic, five-piece set — and many stick to it. Combined with a similarly basic cymbal setup, this is an instrument that will do in a wide variety of styles. A second crash cymbal, to the left of the ride, is often one of the first additions.

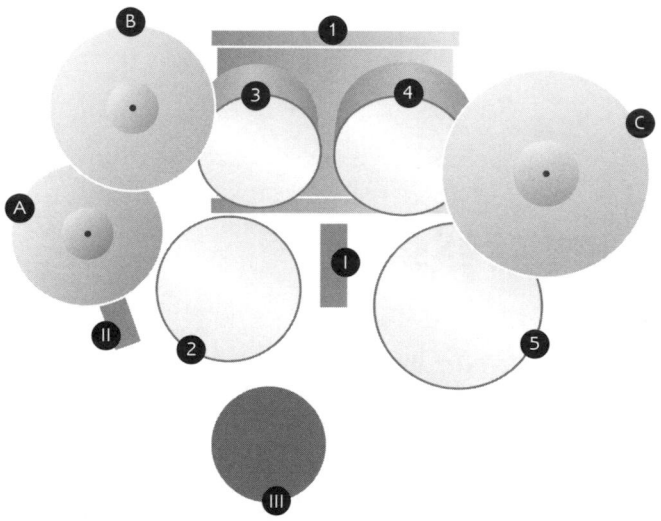

1. 16x22 bass drum	A. 14" hi-hats	I. bass drum pedal
2. 6.5x14 snare drum	B. 16" or 18" crash cymbal	II. hi-hat pedal
3. 10x12 power tom	C. 20" ride cymbal	III. drum throne
4. 11x13 power tom		
5. 16x16 floor tom		

NINE-PIECE ROCK SETUP

The louder the music, the bigger the drums will usually be, and the bigger and heavier the cymbals. Two-ply heads, which dent less easily and produce less overtones, are the most popular choice. The tuning is generally on the low side.

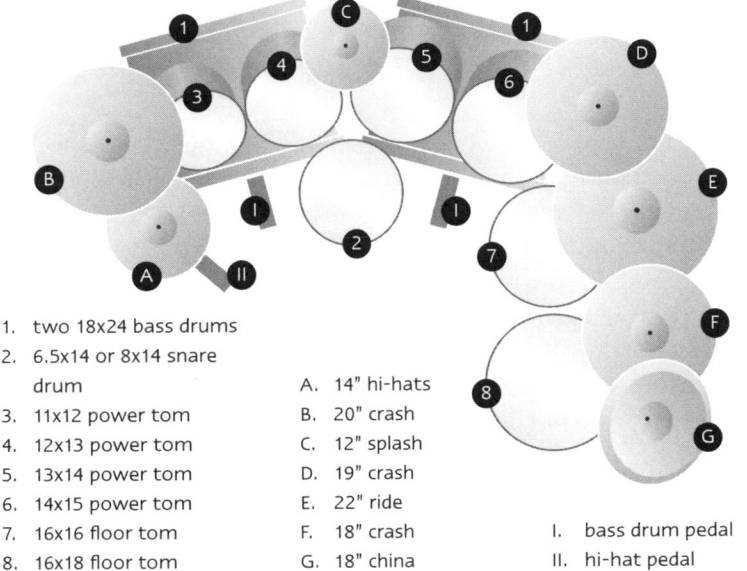

1. two 18x24 bass drums
2. 6.5x14 or 8x14 snare drum
3. 11x12 power tom
4. 12x13 power tom
5. 13x14 power tom
6. 14x15 power tom
7. 16x16 floor tom
8. 16x18 floor tom

A. 14" hi-hats
B. 20" crash
C. 12" splash
D. 19" crash
E. 22" ride
F. 18" crash
G. 18" china

I. bass drum pedal
II. hi-hat pedal

FOUR-PIECE JAZZ SETUP

Many jazz drummers use four-piece sets in small sizes, often combined with two or three fairly thin, big, dark-sounding cymbals that are used both for crashing and timekeeping. One of these cymbals often has three or more rivets. The drums generally have coated, one-ply heads, often tuned to relatively high pitches.

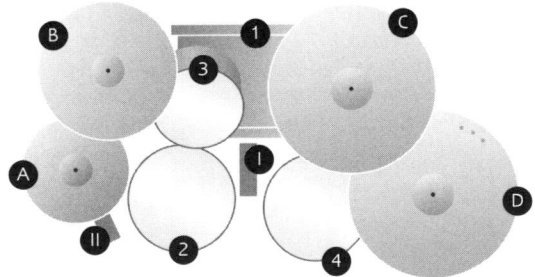

1. 14x18 bass drum
2. 5x14 snare drum
3. 8x12 tom
4. 14x14 floor tom

A. 14" hi-hats
B. 18" or 20" cymbal
C. 22" cymbal
D. 22" sizzle cymbal
   (three rivets)

I. bass drum pedal
II. hi-hat pedal

175

EIGHT-PIECE FUSION SETUP

Fusion is a kind of cross between rock and jazz, and that shows in the typical fusion setup. The drums are smaller than those of the average rock set, but there are more drums than a jazz drummer might use. Similar things can be said about the cymbals and the tuning, both of which are designed to supply a bit more power and definition than jazz drummers normally choose. Heads can be either one or two-ply. Note the second snare, the mounted 'floor' toms, cowbell, double bass drum pedal, and remote hi-hat pedal III, which is used to operate the hi-hat cymbals on the right (G).

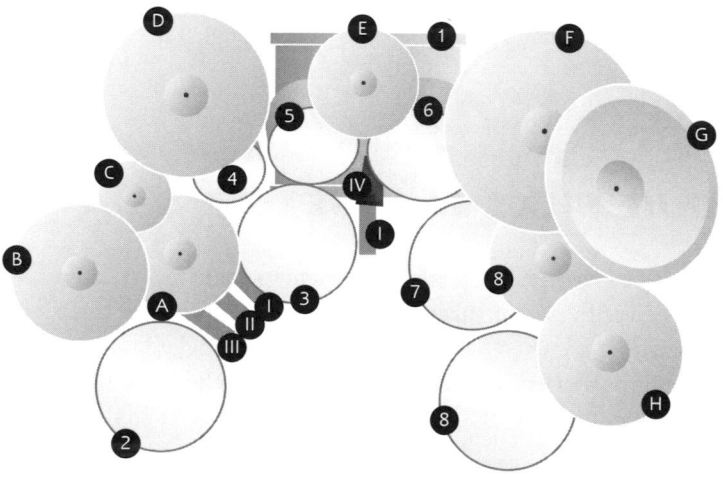

1. 16x20 bass drum	A. 13" hi-hats	I. double pedal
2. 3.5x13 piccolo	B. 15" crash	II. hi-hat pedal
3. 6.5x14 snare drum	C. 8" splash	III. remote hi-hat pedal
4. 7x8 tom	D. 18" crash	IV. cowbell
5. 8x10 tom	E. 12" splash	
6. 9x12 tom	F. 22" ride	
7. 11x14 suspended tom	G. 14" remote hi-hats	
8. 12x15 suspended tom	H. 22" china	
	I. 16" crash	

Glossary

This glossary contains brief definitions and descriptions of the majority of drum set related terms. Most terms are explained in more details as they are introduced in this book. Please consult the index on pages 228–230!

Acousticon
A wood-resin based shell material.

Auxiliary pedal
The 'second' pedal of a double bass drum pedal. See: *Double bass drum pedal.*

Base plate
Stabilizing plate for bass drum and hi-hat pedals.

Bass drum
Your largest drum, played with a bass drum pedal.

Bass drum pedal
The pedal you play the bass drum with. Double pedals allow you to use two feet to play one drum, removing the need for a second bass drum.

Batter head
The top head, i.e. the one you play.

Bead
Another name for the tip of a drum stick.

Bearing edge
The edge of a shell, which 'bears' the head.

Beater
Beats the bass drum. Many drummers use felt beaters; wood or plastic beaters enhance the attack. Double-sided beaters usually have one soft (felt) and one hard (wood or plastic) side.

Bell
Alternative name for cymbal cup.

Boom stand
Stand with an extra, adjustable arm (the boom). Sometimes equipped?? with a (removable) counter weight for additional stability. Telescopic boom arms provide extra reach. Convertible boom stands can be converted into a straight stand.

Bracket
The arms of a tom holder and the legs of a floor tom are held in place with brackets.

Brushes
Brushing your drum heads with the steel or nylon strands of a pair of brushes or *wire brushes* produces a shhhhh sound. Available in telescopic and non-telescopic models.

Chinese cymbal
Cymbal with a turned-up edge and a square cup. Also available in numerous Western variations.

Clutch
Secures your top hi-hat cymbal to the pull rod.

Concert toms
Single-headed toms; also known as melodic toms.

Counter hoop
See: *Hoop.*

Crash, crash cymbal
Fast-speaking cymbals that sound just like their name; mainly used for accenting and adding color to the music.

Cup
The little 'bulge' in the middle of a cymbal, also known as the bell, often used for penetrating ride patterns in Latin rhythms.

Cymbals
Deceptively simple-looking discs, usually made of bronze, available in numerous sizes, shapes, types, and thicknesses.

Dampening
See: *Muffling*.

Dot
A thin, circular piece of drum head material, stuck on a drum head. Dries out the sound and helps resist denting. Some snare drum heads have a dot on the reverse side.

Double-braced
Double-braced stands have legs that are made up of two metal strips, instead of one.

Double bass drum pedal
Features two footboards and two beaters so you can play your single bass drum with two feet.

Drop-lock clutch
Type of clutch that allows you to 'drop' the top cymbal onto the bottom cymbal. This allows you to play double bass drum patterns with a closed hi-hat sound.

Drum key
T-shaped tool for tuning drums; also available in speed versions and ratchet versions.

Drum machine
Programmable electronic 'drum set' or drum computer.

Drum rack
Replaces the bottom sections of cymbal stands, microphone stands, and so on. Especially useful for larger setups.

Electronic drums
A series of pads with built-in triggers that activate digitally recorded sounds (*samples*) in the instrument's sound module.

Flesh hoop
The (typically aluminum) hoop of a drum head.

Floating heads
Drums with slightly undersized shells have floating heads. Most drums do.

Floor tom
Three-legged drum, most popular in 16x16.

Flush bracing
See: *Lugs*.

Fusion set
Fusion is a musical mixture of rock and jazz elements, which led to the creation of the fusion drum set, usually featuring 10" and 12" rack toms and one or two suspended 'floor' toms.

Hardware
Stands, pedals, holders, and racks, plus the lugs, tension rods, washers,

179

bolts and all other metal items — except for the cymbals.

Heads

Drum heads are made of one or two thin plies of polyester film, the sound being determined by their thickness and by additional coatings, dots, fillings, holes and/or built-in muffling rings, to name just a few. Most drums have two heads: a top or batter head and a bottom or resonant head (called snare-side head on snare drums; front head on bass drums).

Hickory

Most popular type of wood for sticks (and hammer handles, and hockey sticks…)

High-tension lugs

See: *Lugs*.

Hi-hat

Two (hi-hat) cymbals of equal size and a (hi-hat) stand with a pedal that operates them.

Hoop

Drums are tuned by using the hoops to tighten the head over the shell. Also known as counter hoops. See also: *Flesh hoop, Triple-flanged hoops*.

Isolated mounting system

Isolates drums (rack toms, especially) from their mounting hardware, enhancing their sound and resonance. Introduced by Gary Gauger. His RIMS are regarded as one of the few major innovations in drums in recent decades.

Key bolts, key rods

See: *Tension rods*.

Lathed cymbals

Most cymbals are lathed. The lathing knife creates the circular pattern of grooves on the cymbal's surface, opening up its sound. Unlathed cymbals have a tighter sound.

Lug bolts

See: *Tension rods*.

Lugs, lug casings

Metal casings which house the lug nuts into which the tension rods are screwed. Also known as tension mounts. If a drum is said to have flush bracing, long lugs, double lugs, or high-tension lugs, this means that each lug receives a tension rod from both the batter and the resonant head. See also: Nodal points.

Mallets

Sticks with large heads, usually covered with felt (tympani mallets) or wound with yarn (xylophone mallets, for instance). People who 'play mallets', play mallet instruments such as the vibraphone and the marimba.

Melodic toms

See: *Concert toms*.

Memory locks

Metal clamps that help you set up fast. Originally a trade name; other names include *key locks* and *stop locks*.

180

Muffling
There are many different ways of muffling or dampening your drums, which controls the tone to some extent.

Multi-clamp
Used to clamp holders to stands or racks.

Mylar
Widely-used (Dupont) trade name for the polyester film that most drum heads are made of.

Nodal points
Drum shells are said to have nodal points, indicating positions at which there is no vibration. It is claimed that mounting lugs and brackets on those spots enhances the drum's resonance. Not all experts agree on this issue — but what else is new...

Offset tilter
Offers maximum positioning and makes packing easier.

Oil
Two-ply heads often look as though they have oil between the plies. Most of them don't however. The colorful effects you may see when looking through a two-ply drum head are known as Newton rings, interference patterns that appear when light is reflected as it passes through the two transparent plies of the drum head.

O-ring
Ring cut out of the film that drum heads are made of. Popular for

muffling snare drums.

Pad
The most basic practice pad is a wooden plank with a slice of rubber on top, enabling silent practice. See also: *Electronic drums.*

Ported bass drum head
Bass drum front head with a hole for sound and/or miking purposes. The smaller and the more off-center the hole is, the less it will affect the sound.

Power toms
Toms with extra deep shells. Like 'power' cymbals, they're primarily designed for heavy players.

Practice pad
See: *Pad.*

Pull rod
The rod to which you attach the top cymbal of your hi-hat. It 'pulls' the top down towards the bottom cymbal.

Rack
Drum rack; hardware system that replaces the bottom sections of cymbal stands and other stands.

Rack toms
Common name for the smaller toms, which are mounted on the bass drum or on a drum rack.

Reinforcement hoops
Wooden rings around the inside edges of a drum. They reinforce the shell and also influence the sound.

181

Remote hi-hat
Hi-hat pedal with a long cable connecting the pedal to the top section. Often used for a second pair of hi-hat cymbals on the right side of the set. See also: *X-hat*.

Resonant head
The bottom head. See: *Heads*.

Ride cymbal
Usually the heaviest and largest cymbal of the set, primarily used for timekeeping —you play time (the ride) on it.

RIMS
See: *Isolated mounting system*.

Rivets
Inserting one or more rivets into a cymbal will turn it into a sizzle cymbal.

Seamless shells
Some metal snare shells and counter hoops are seamless, meaning their shape is forced out of a flat metal disc, thus eliminating the need for a welded seam.

Self-muffled head
Head with built-in muffling.

Shell
The sound chamber of a drum. If you take every single component (heads, lugs, etc.) off your drum, all you'll be left with is the shell.

Shell set, shell kit, shell pack
A set sold without any stands or pedals.

Single lugs
See: *Lugs*.

Sizzle cymbal
Cymbal with rivets, producing a 'sizzling' sound.

Snare, snare drum
One of the two main drums of the drum set. Both the drum's name and its sound come from the snappy snares that are stretched across the bottom head.

Snare bed
Snare drums are a bit shallower where the snare strings or straps run over the edge. This recess, referred to as the snare bed, helps the snares to lie flat against the snare-side head over their entire length.

Snare-side head
Bottom head of a snare drum. Very, very thin.

Snare strainer
Mechanism that allows you to adjust the tension of the snares, and to disengage them (throw them off) if you wish. Other names include *snare mechanism*, and *throw-off*.

Snappy snares, snares
The spiraled wires (about twenty of them) that are stretched across the bottom (snare-side) head.

Spring tension
Determines how heavy or light a pedal feels. Adjustable on all bass drum pedals and most hi-hat pedals.

Square drum sizes
Drums whose depth equals their diameter (e.g., 12x12).

Stands
You use a variety of stands for toms, cymbals, and snare drums, with single or double-braced legs.

Suspended cymbal
Symphonic cymbal, mounted on a stand.

Symmetrical drum sizes
See: *Square drum sizes.*

Tension mounts
See: *Lugs.*

Tension rods, tension screws, tension bolts
Variety of names for the 'tuning keys' of a drum. Also known as key rods, lug bolts, or key bolts.

Throne
Drum throne, drum stool.

Throw-off
See: *Snare strainer.*

Tilter
Enables a part of a stand to tilt. You'll find a tilter on all cymbal stands, snare drum stands, tom, and hi-hat pedals. Ratchet tilters or gear tilters use two sets of interlocking teeth; toothless tilters allow for finer adjustment.

Tips
Most drum sticks have wooden tips or beads, in a wide variety of shapes and sizes. Nylon tips sound brighter, especially on cymbals.

Tom holder, tom mount
Mount for rack toms.

Tom, tom toms
The 'other' drums, besides your snare drum and bass drum. May either be mounted (rack toms) or on legs (floor toms).

Trigger pad
Drum pad with built-in electronics that pick up your beats and send them to the sound module where they trigger sounds. See also: *Electronic drums, Pad.*

Triple-flanged hoops
Pressed hoops usually have three flanges.

Tuning
Some say you can't tune a drum; all you can do is tighten the heads — but most drummers do use the word tuning.

Vent hole
A small hole in the drum shell, allowing the air to escape from within the drum as you hit it.

Wire brushes
See: *Brushes.*

X-hat
Holder for an extra pair of hi-hat cymbals, originally a trade name. See also: *Remote hi-hat.*

TIPCODE LIST

The Tipcodes in this book offer easy access to short movies, photo series, soundtracks, and other additional information at www.tipbook.com. For your convenience, the Tipcodes in this Tipbook have been listed below.

Tipcode	Topic	Chapter	Page
DRUM-001	A five-piece drum set, step by step	2	6
DRUM-002	Basic rock rhythm (audio)	3	20
DRUM-003	Checking the bearing edge	5	44
DRUM-004	Checking the diameter	5	45
DRUM-005	Tom holder w. ball-and-socket joint	5	59
DRUM-006	Setting a memory lock	5	59
DRUM-007	Spring adjustment bass drum pedal	6	68
DRUM-008	Spring adjustment hi-hat pedal	6	74
DRUM-009	Boom stand	6	80
DRUM-010	Adjusting a snare drum stand	6	81
DRUM-011	Removing a muffling ring	7	89
DRUM-012	Lathed/unlathed cymbals	9	105
DRUM-013	Ratchet key	10	117
DRUM-014	Removing drum head (two keys)	10	119
DRUM-015	Basic drum head tension	10	119
DRUM-016	Tuning order	10	119
DRUM-017	Fine tuning	10	122
DRUM-018	Making a bridge for the snares	10	126
DRUM-019	Adjusting an internal muffler	10	135
DRUM-020	Top cymbal and clutch	11	140
DRUM-021	Adjusting the clutch	11	140
DRUM-022	Making of a drum	14	158
DRUM-023	Making of a cymbal	14	159

Want to know more?

This book gives you all the basics you need for buying, maintaining, tuning, and using drums, cymbals, sticks and drum heads. If you want to know more, check out the magazines, books and websites listed below.

Magazines and e-zines

There are a number of specialized drummers' magazines and e-zines, featuring interviews, product reviews and other articles. You may also find relevant articles in general music magazines.

- *Modern Drummer*, www.moderndrummer.com.
- *Drum!*, www.drummagazine.com
- *DrumPRO Magazine*, drumpro.com (e-zine)
- *Traps, The Art Of Drumming*, www.trapsmagazine.com
- *Tom Girl Magazine*, www.tomgirlmagazine.com (e-zine)
- *Percussive Notes*, www.pas.org/publications/notes.cfm
- *Not So Modern Drummer*, www.notsomoderndrummer.com
- *Classic Drummer*, www.classicdrummer.com
- *Muzik Etc./Drums Etc.* (Canada), www.muziketc.ca
- *Rhythm* (UK), www.futurenet.com
- *Drummer Magazine* (UK), www.drummer-mag.com

Books

Many books on drums deal largely with the history of the instrument; other publications cover today's drum sets as well. The following list contains examples of both.

- *The Drumset Owner's Manual— A Heavily Illustrated Guide To Selecting, Setting Up And Maintaining All Components Of The Acoustic Drumset*, by Ronald Vaughan (McFarland & Company, 1993; 164 pages; ISBN 0-89950-755-7)

- *The Drum Handbook — Buying, Maintaining, And Getting The Best From Your Drum Kit*, Geoff Nichols (Backbeat Books, 2003; 192 pages; ISBN 0-87930-750-1)

- *The Cymbal Book*, by Hugo Pinksterboer (Hal Leonard, 1993; 212 pages; ISBN 0-7935-1920-9)

- *The Drummer's Almanac*, by Jon Cohan (Hal Leonard, 1998; 80 pages; ISBN 0-7935-6696-7)

- *The Drummer's Studio Survival Guide*, by Mark Huntley Parsons (Modern Drummer Publications, 1996; 94 pages; ISBN 0-7935-7222-3)

- *Guide to Vintage Drums*, by John Aldridge (Centerstream, USA, 1996; 174 pages; ISBN 0-9317-5979-X)

- *Gretsch Drums — The Legacy of That Great Gretsch Sound*, by Chet Falzerano (Centerstream, 1996; 144 pages; ISBN 0-9317-5998-6)

- *History Of Leedy Drum Co.*: The World's Largest Drum Co., by Rob Cook (Centerstream, 1996; 178 pages; ISBN 0-9317-5974-9)

- *Star Sets: Drum Kits Of The Great Drummers*, by Jon Cohan (Hal Leonard, 1995; 160 pages; ISBN 0-7935-3489-5)

- *The Drum Book, A History Of The Rock Drum Kit*, by Geoff Nichols (Balafon, 1997; 112 pages; ISBN 1-8715-4725-3)

- *The Great American Drums And The Companies That Made Them*, 1920–1969, by Harry Cangany (Hal Leonard, 1996; 72 pages; ISBN 0-7935-6356-9)

Internet

The Internet is an excellent source of information on instruments and drummers. Here are some websites to start with:
- www.drummergirl.com
- www.drummerszone.com
- www.drummerworld.com
- www.drums.com
- www.drumset.com
- www.drum-talk.com
- www.drumtips.com
- Percussion Information: www.xs4all.nl/~marcz

Also check out the websites of the drummer's magazines listed above!

Looking for a teacher?

The Internet can also help you find a teacher. Search for "drum teacher" and the name of area or city where you live, or visit one of the following special interest websites:
- PrivateLessons.com: www.privatelessons.com
- MusicStaff.com: www.musicstaff.com
- The Music Teachers List: www.teachlist.com
- Private Music Instructor National Directory: www.oberwerk.com/pmind

187

Tipbook rudiments and drum beats

The previous chapters of this book are intended to make you want to get up and play the instrument. On the following pages, you'll find a variety of drum rudiments and a large number of basic and advanced drum beats in a wide variety of musical styles. Enjoy!

RUDIMENTS

The rudiments are basic sticking patterns, which can be applied in a wide variety of styles of music. Mastering the rudiments improves your stick dexterity, and it allows you — for example — to change sticking directions to reverse your movement around the drum set. Also, rudiments allow you to change the sound of the instrument: Playing a single stroke roll on a drum (LRLR) sounds very different from playing a paradiddle (LRLL) or a double stroke roll (RRLL) on that same drum, even when played at the same tempo and volume level!

Practicing rudiments

Most methods suggest that you practice rudiments slow to fast to slow (start slow, then speed up, the slow down again), and also to play them at various steady tempos. Tempo ranges have been specified for some of the rudiments on the following pages.

Roll rudiments

Single stroke rolls

1. **Single stroke roll**

```
R  L  R  L  R  L  R  L
L  R  L  R  L  R  L  R
```

Double stroke open rolls

2. **Double stroke open roll**
   (long roll)

```
R  R  L  L  R  R  L  L
L  L  R  R  L  L  R  R
```

3. **Five stroke roll** (168–184)

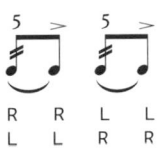

```
R     R     L     L
L     L     R     R
```

4. **Seven stroke roll**

```
L     R     L     R
R     L     R     L
```

5. **Nine stroke roll**

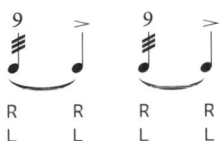

```
R     R     R     R
L     L     L     L
```

6. **Ten stroke roll**

```
L     L  R  L     L  R
R     R  L  R     R  L
```

7. **Eleven stroke roll**

```
L     L  R  L     L  R
R     R  L  R     R  L
```

8. **Thirteen stroke roll**

```
R     R  L     L
L     L  R     R
```

9. **Fifteen stroke roll**

```
L     R  L     R
R     L  R     L
```

Diddle rudiments / paradiddles

10. Single paradiddle *(160–200)*

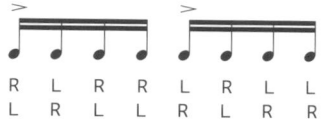

R L R R L R L L
L R L L R L R R

11. Double paradiddle *(108–120)*

R L R L R R L R L R L L

Flam rudiments

12. Flam *(168–176)*

L R R L
R L L R

13. Flam accent *(168–184)*

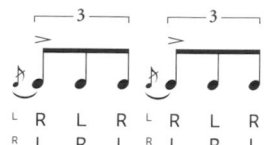

L R L R L R L R
R L R L R L R L

---

14. Flam tap

L R R R L L L R R R L L
R L L L R R R L L L R R

15. Flamacue *(126–152)*

L R L R L L R
R L R L R R L

---

16. Flam paradiddle *(120–132)*

L R L R R R L R L L
R L R L L L R L R R

17. Flam paradiddlediddle

L R L R R L L R L R L L R R
R L R L L R R L R L R R L L

Drag rudiments

18. Drag *(a.k.a. Ruff)*

L L R R R L

19. Single drag

R L L R L R R L

20. **Double drag**

L L R   L L R L   R R L   R R L R

21. **Lesson 25** (126–132)

R R L   R L   L L R   L R

22. **Drag paradiddle #1** (84–96)

R L L R L R R L R R L R L L

23. **Drag paradiddle #2**

R L L R L L R L R R L R R L R R L R L L

24. **Single ratamacue**

L L R L R L   R R L R L R

25. **Double ratamacue**

L L R L L R L R L R R L R R L R L R

26. **Triple ratamacue**

L L R L L R L L R L R L   R R L R R L R R L R L R

Seven essential rudiments

The seven essential rudiments are the seven rudiments you need
to master in order to perform the other rudiments. They are the
single stroke roll, the multiple bounce roll (not listed above), the
double stroke open roll, the five stroke roll, the single paradiddle,
the flam, and the drag. The long roll or double stroke open roll is
also referred to as 'mammy-daddy', 'ma ma da da', or 'ma ma pa pa'.

193

More rudiments

There are many more rudiments than the ones listed on the previous pages. The list of Percussive Arts Society International Drum Rudiments (PAS, www.pas.org) consists of forty rudiments, including the twenty-six original rudiments listed above. Below are some examples of other rudiments.

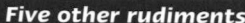

Five other rudiments

Single stroke four

Triple stroke roll

Triple paradiddle

Paradiddlediddle

Inverted flam tap

Thirteen to twenty-six

Originally, there were thirteen rudiments only, originated by the National Association of Rudimental Drummers in 1933. In later years, a second set of thirteen rudiments was added to the original thirteen 'essential' rudiments. Lesson 25 was the 25th rudiment of this list of twenty-six.

(Non-)alternating rudiments

Note that some of the rudiments are alternating; others are non-alternating. When playing alternating or hand-to-hand-

rudiments (e.g., the five stroke roll), you will automatically start with your right hand and your left hand alternately. Traditionally, drummers always start the non-alternating rudiments with the left hand; this would help them develop this — typically weaker – hand. You can also practice these rudiments starting with your right hand, as the sticking suggests, as well as alternating.

BASIC BEATS

Following are some popular drum set beats in a variety of musical styles. Note that this is not intended to be a course in drumming, and that there are many drum books available that show you how to play numerous other rhythms and grooves. *Tip:* a good teacher will help you make these grooves sound great!

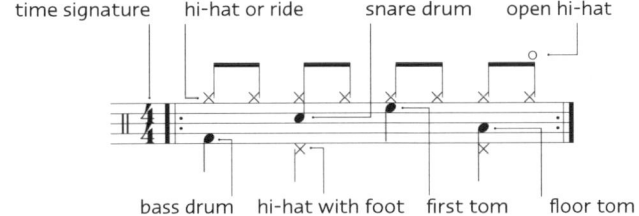

Drum key.

ROCK

Many of the rock beats below can be used in a wide variety of rock related styles, from soul and funk to gospel and fusion. The first beats in this section are very basic and straightforward.

Hi-hat or ride
You can play all rock grooves either on your hi-hat or on your ride cymbal. If you use the latter, you may play the hi-hat pedal with your foot on counts 2 and 4, or on counts 1, 2, 3, and 4, for

195

example. For more projection, use the cup of the ride cymbal. For a looser, sizzling, trashy, sustaining sound, play the hi-hat with the cymbals partially open.

Backbeats

In most rock oriented styles, you will accent the backbeats (usually 2 and 4) on the snare drum. Other snare drum notes are usually ghost notes, played very softly.

Eighth-note ride patterns

The following one bar phrases have the snare drum on 2 and 4.

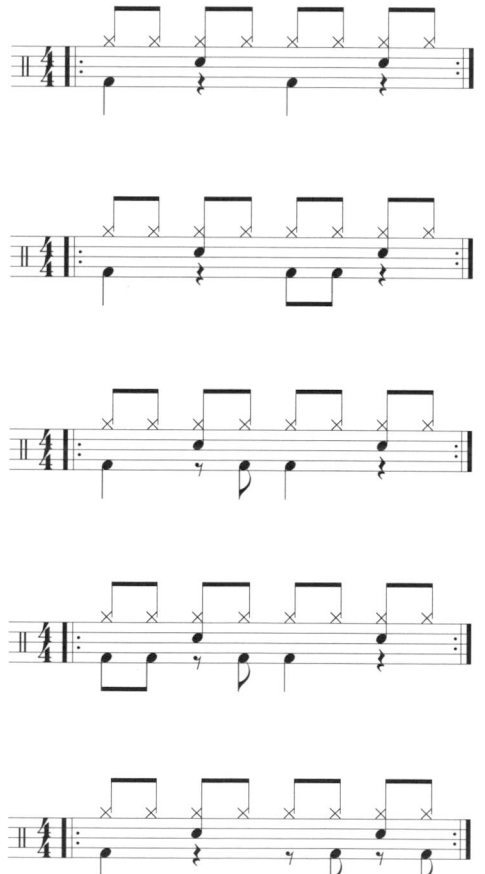

Eighth-note ride patterns

Here are some two bar phrases, again with the snare drum on 2 and 4.

Snare on 4 or 3

The snare drum can also be played on 4 only, and some songs ask for a snare drum on 3.

Snare drum variations

More snare drum variations. Also try playing some of the snare drum notes on a tom tom, for example the last two eighth notes of the first example

Break up the ride

Provide a song with a different feeling by skipping the hi-hat or the ride cymbal when you hit your snare drum — every time...

... or on the 4 of every other bar. Play the accented note on a half-open hi-hat, for example.

Quarter-note ride pattern

Instead of eighth notes, you can play quarter notes on the ride cymbal. Using your pedal or playing the snare drum without playing the ride or your hi-hat at the same time, may take some practice. Next to playing the following examples, you can substitute the eighth note patterns in all the grooves above for quarter note patterns too.

200

Sixteenth-note patterns

Create yet another feel by playing sixteenth notes on the hi-hat or the ride. This makes playing sixteenth notes on the bass drum and the snare drum a little easier too, as these notes are supported by the ride pattern.

Sixteenth-note patterns for higher tempos

To play sixteenth-note grooves at higher tempos, use alternating hands on the hi-hat. You can play the grooves on the previous page that way, of course: Simply leave out the hi hat where you're supposed to play the snare drum. Or check out the following grooves:

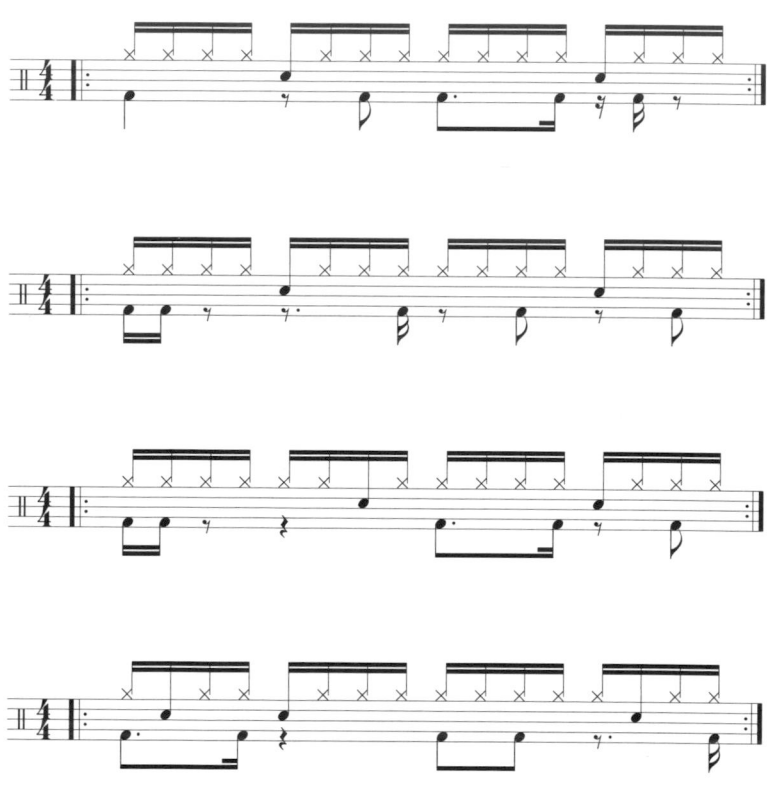

Tip: Also try playing these and similar patterns with your left hand on the hi-hat and your right hand on (the bell of) your ride cymbal.

Sixteenth notes on bass and snare drum

Combining an eighth or quarter note ride pattern with sixteenth notes on the bass drum and the snare drum offers numerous new possibilities, both in $\frac{4}{4}$ and $\frac{3}{4}$ — and in any other time signature.

The second eighth note

Basically, all grooves on the previous pages can be played with either quarter notes, eighth notes or sixteenth notes on the hi-hat or the ride. Another popular variation is to play the second eighth note only. Consider closing your hi-hat on every beat, as suggested in the following examples.

Ride cymbal accents

Rather than playing the second eighth note only, you can accent that note and play the downbeats (1, 2, 3, 4) softly.
Tip: Also do this the other way around, *i.e.*, play the eighth note grooves earlier in this chapter while accenting the downbeats, and playing the upbeats softly, as follows:

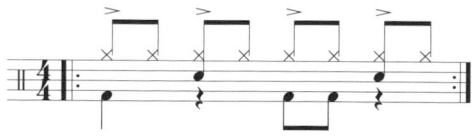

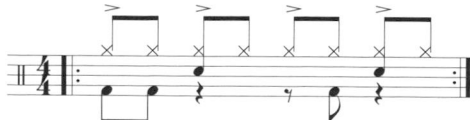

Expand your repertoire

Expand your repertoire by interchanging the snare drum and the bass drum on some notes: Compare each groove A to groove B.

A

B

A

B

The second approach is to make small rhytmical variations.

A

B

Ride patterns

Of course, all grooves on the previous pages can be played with a quarter note pulse on the hi-hat or the ride cymbal, or with an eighth note pulse, or sixteenths. You can also play them with the ride beats shown in the following two examples:

Breath some extra air into the music by opening up the hi-hat on every upbeat, or make for a different timbre by using your ride cymbal instead of the hi-hat.

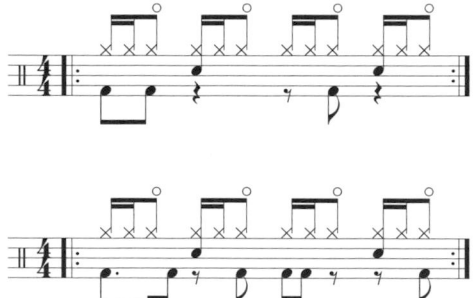

Introducing triplets

Using triplets in rock beats can make for very smooth grooves. Play the triplet notes very softly.

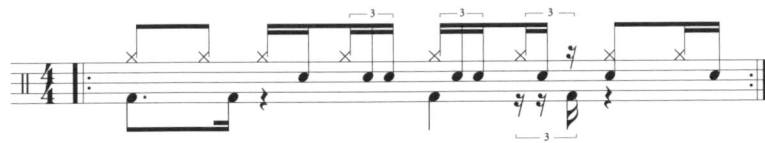

Odd time signatures

Most rock songs are in $\frac{4}{4}$ (common time), and others in $\frac{3}{4}$, but you may come across songs in $\frac{5}{4}$ or $\frac{7}{4}$ as well.

DRUM BEATS

Most of the grooves on the previous pages can be used in a variety of musical styles, from straight ahead rock and hard rock to funk, fusion and country. On the next pages are some examples of specific grooves per style.

Metal

Modern metal grooves are characterized by their busy, syncopated bass drum patterns. To be played loud, and often with a partially open hi-hat. Higher tempos than (hard) rock.

Metal

Speed metal tempos require easier grooves.

Metal

Speed metal

209

Disco

Disco

Disco asks for very basic beats with a four on the floor bass drum pattern, and often an open hi-hat on the upbeats.

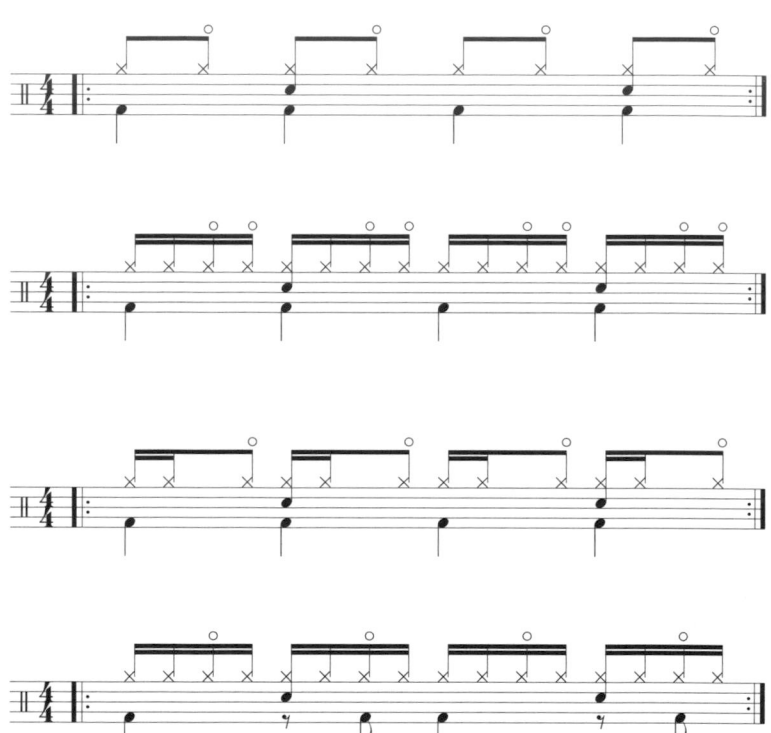

Funk

Funk

Funk blends elements from rhythm & blues, soul, and rock. Very basic rock groove can be really effective (use a high pitched snare sound!), but funk grooves often incorporate syncopated snare and bass drum patterns.

Hip hop

Hip hop grooves are related to funk grooves.

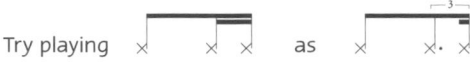

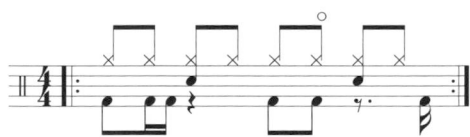

House

Like disco, house beats often use a four on the floor bass drum, and a hi-hat that often opens on the upbeats.

House

Hip house is a bit faster, so use simple rhythms.

House

Soca house mixes house beats with the Caribbean soca rhythm. The groove below is used in traditional soca too.

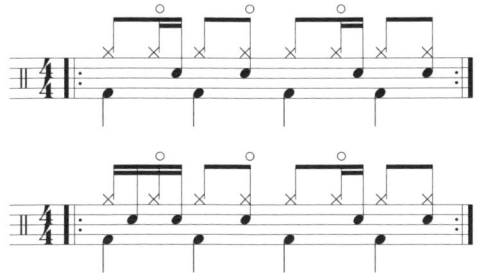

House

Hip house

Soca house

213

New Jack Swing

New Jack Swing is a hip-hop groove with syncopated bass and snare hits that stem from the be-bop era. Play this half-time shuffle on the hi-hat – but try your ride cymbal as well.

Reggae

In reggae, you'll often hear the snare drum (and the bass drum) on three.

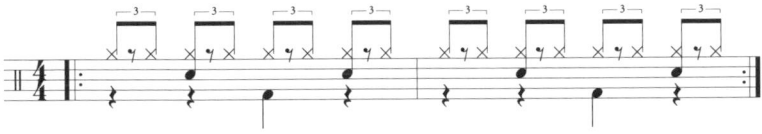

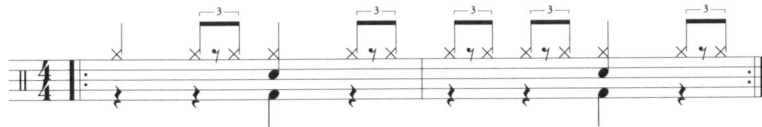

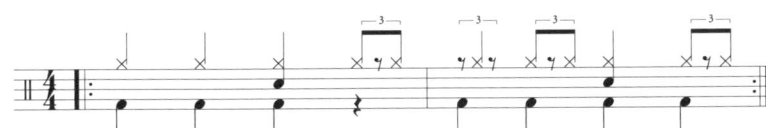

Motown

Motown

Many Motown-songs use a quarter note snare drum beat, like this:

Country

In country, drummers often play rim clicks (a.k.a. cross-stick rim shots). The second 'country' groove is identical to a popular punk groove – apart from the tempo, the sound, and the intensity.

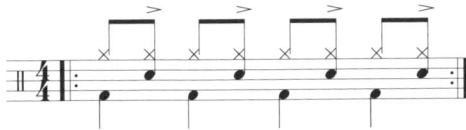

The so-called train beat is also used in rock and other styles.

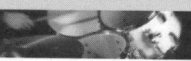

Shuffles & Blues

Shuffles & Blues

Shuffle beats are often used in the blues, but also in early rock 'n roll songs, in zydeco, country, and other styles. The snare drum gets an accent on 2 and 4, of course.

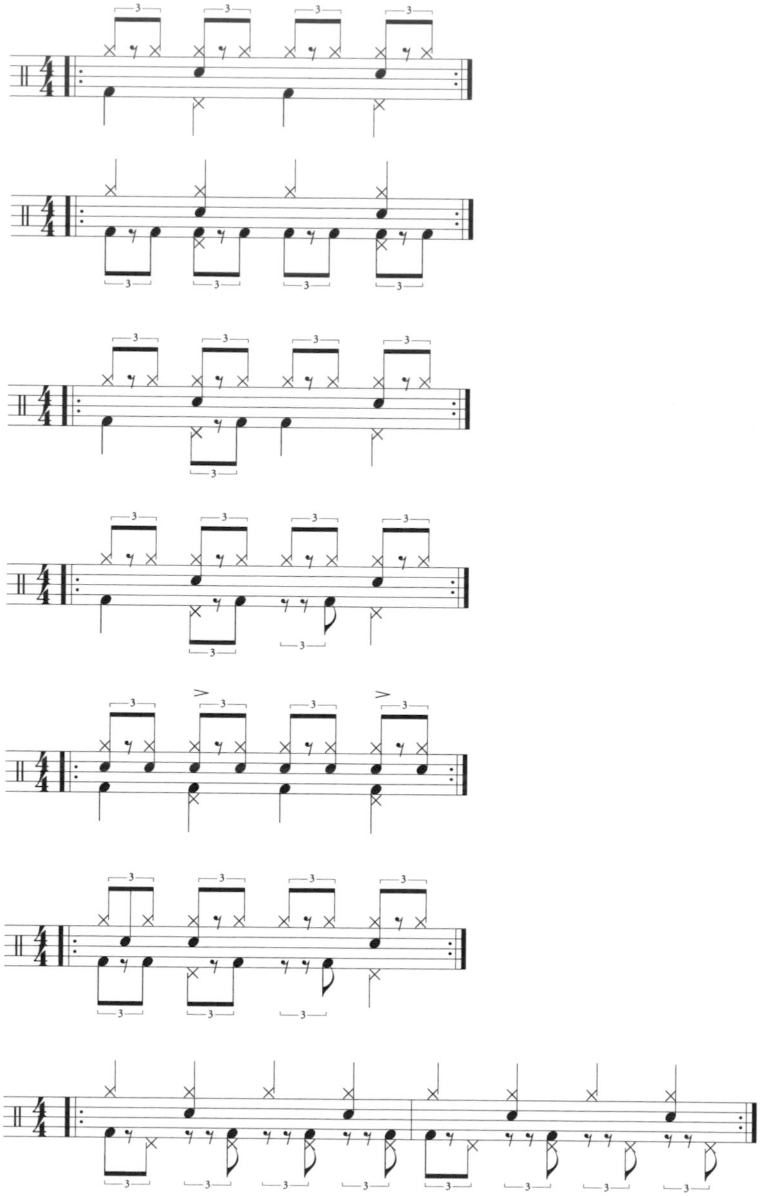

Slow blues

Blues

Slow blues songs are often in $\frac{12}{8}$. The sixteenth-note cymbal variations can be played as triplets too!

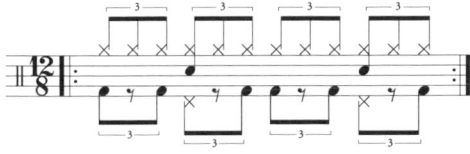

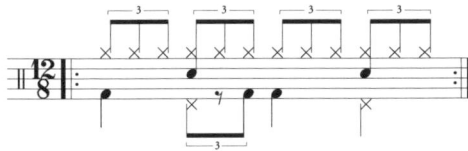

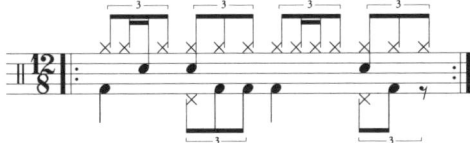

Jazz

All of the grooves on the previous pages are supposed to be repeated throughout (a part of) the song you're playing. Jazz drummers, on the contrary, typically play something different in every bar, inspired by or responding to the song or to the soloist who's playing. The following eight bar fantasy shows the standard ride pattern (first two bars) and some of the millions of ride, snare and bass drum variations. The hi-hat is typically – but certainly not always – closed on 2 and 4.

Odd time Jazz

Jazz

There are many jazz standards in $\frac{3}{4}$ and much less in $\frac{5}{4}$, $\frac{7}{4}$, and other odd time signatures.

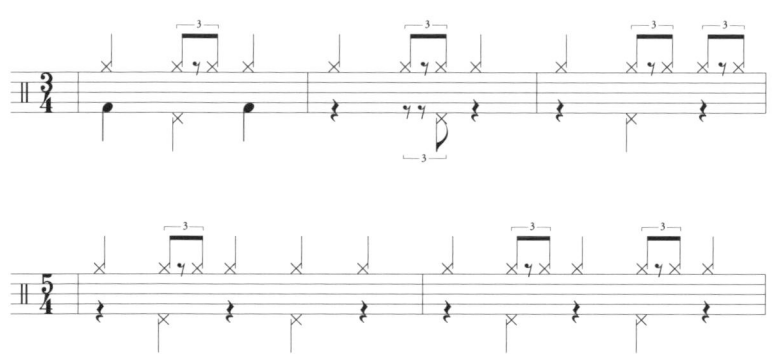

Rhumba

Latin

Traditionally, latin music does not use a drum set – but many latin rhythms have been adapted to the instrument.

The rhumba is from Cuba.

Mambo

Latin

Here are two basic mambo beats.

Songo

Latin

Contrary to most latin rhythms, the songo was created for the drum set.

Latin

Three Afro-Cuban grooves in ⁶⁄₈. The third one is a very busy, driving nañigo. ³⁄₄

Afro-Cuban ⁶⁄₈

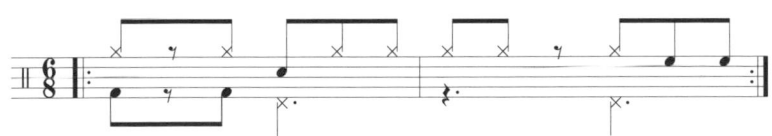

223

Bossa nova

Brazilian

The two most popular Brazilian styles of music are the bossa nova and the samba.

The sound of the bossa nova requires you to play rim clicks on the snare drum, as indicated. Try reversing the order of the two bars in each groove. Play the ride pattern on your hi-hat or your ride cymbal, or use a brush on your snare drum, or try playing a shaker instead! Splashing you hi-hat on 1 or 3, for example, adds a nice effect.

rim click

224

Samba

Brazilian

There are a thousand ways to play the samba on the drum set. Here are just a few of them. Note that the hi-hat can be played on 2 and 4 or 1 and 3. Use the last groove if the tempo is really high. The snare drum patterns give here can of course be used with any of the ride patterns.

ESSENTIAL DATA

In the event of your equipment being stolen or lost, or if you decide to sell it, it's useful to have all the relevant data at hand. Here are two pages to make those notes. For the insurance, for the police, or just for yourself.

INSURANCE

Insurance company:

Phone: Email:

Broker:

Phone: Email:

Policy no.:

Premium:

DRUM SET

Make and series:

Color:

Price:

Date of purchase:

Place of purchase:

Phone: Email:

DRUMS

1

2

3

4

5

6

7

8

9

10

11

226 12

CYMBALS

Brand name, series, size, date of purchase, price, serial number, and/or other data per cymbal. Most cymbals come without a serial number. If it's there, you'll find it on the inside of the cup.

1
2
3
4
5
6
7
8
9
10

ACCESSORIES AND OTHER INSTRUMENTS

1
2
3
4
5
6
7
8

ADDITIONAL NOTES

INDEX

Please check out the glossary on pages 177-183 for additional definitions of the terms used in this book.

THE TIPBOOK SERIES

Did you enjoy Tipbook Drums? There are also Tipbooks for your fellow band and orchestra members! Tipbook Drums is just one of the many volumes of the international Tipbook Series. The series is comprised of eleven books on musical instruments, including the singing voice, in addition to Tipbook Music on Paper, Tipbook Amplifiers and Effects, and Tipbook Music for Kids and Teens – a Guide for Parents.

Every Tipbook is a highly accessible and easy-to-read compilation of the knowledge and expertise of numerous musicians, teachers, technicians, and other experts, written for musicians of all ages, at all levels, and in any style of music.

Tipbook Music on Paper

Tipbook Music on Paper – Basic Theory offers everything you need to read and understand the language of music. The book presumes no prior understanding of theory and begins with the basics, explaining standard notation, but moves on to advanced topics such as odd time signatures and transposing music in a fashion that makes things really easy to understand. It's also a handy reference, and the 4"x8" Tipbook format allows you to take it anywhere you go.

Instrument Tipbooks

The Instrument Tipbooks each offer a wealth of highly accessible, yet well-founded information on one or more closely related instruments. The first chapters of each Tipbook explain the very basics of the instrument(s), explaining all the parts and what they do, describing what's involved in learning to play, and indicating typical instrument prices. The core chapters, addressed to advanced players as well, turn you into an instant expert on the instrument. This knowledge allows you to make an informed purchase and get the most out of your instrument. Comprehensive chapters on maintenance, intonation, and tuning are also included, as well a brief section on the history, the family, and the production of the instrument.

231

Tipbook Violin and Viola, Tipbook Cello

The Tipbooks on orchestral strings cover a wide range of subjects, ranging from an explanation of different types of tuning pegs, fine tuners, and tailpieces, to how body dimensions and the bridge may influence the instrument's timbre. Tips on how to audition instruments and bows are included. Special chapters are dedicated to the characteristics of different types of strings, bows, and rosins, allowing you to get the most out of the instrument.

Tipbook Piano

Choosing a piano becomes a lot easier with the knowledge provided in *Tipbook Piano*, which makes for a better understanding of this complex, expensive instrument without going into too much detail. How to judge and compare piano keyboards and pedals, the influence of the instrument's dimensions, different types of cabinets, how to judge an instrument's timbre, the difference between laminated and solid wood soundboards, accessories, hybrid and digital pianos, and why tuning and regulation are so important: Everything is covered in this handy guide.

Tipbook Acoustic Guitar

Tipbook Acoustic Guitar explains all elements you recognize and judge a guitar's timbre, performance, and playability. Of course there are dedicated chapters on different types of strings and their characteristics, on changing and cleaning strings, on tuning, and even on how to best maintain your fingernails.

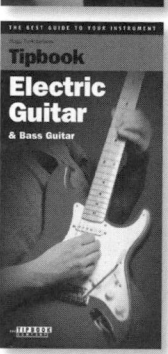

Tipbook Electric Guitar & Bass Guitar

Electric guitars and bass guitars come in many shapes and sizes. *Tipbook Electric Guitar & Bass Guitar* explains all their features and characteristics, from neck profiles, frets, and types of wood to different types of pickups, tuning machines, and — of course — strings. Tuning and advanced do-it-yourself intonation techniques are included.

Tipbook Flute & Piccolo

Flute prices range from a few hundred to fifty thousand dollars and more. *Tipbook Flute and Piccolo* tells you how workmanship, materials, and other elements make for different instruments with vastly different prices, and teaches you how to find the instrument that best suits your or your child's needs. Open-hole or closed-hole keys, a B-foot or a C-foot, split-E or donut, inline or offset G? You'll be able to answer all these questions — and more — after reading this guide.

Tipbook Clarinet

Tipbook Clarinet sheds light on every element of this fascinating instrument. The knowledge presented in this guide makes selecting and auditioning a clarinet much easier, and it turns you into an instant expert on the pros and cons of offset and in-line trill keys, rounded or French-style keys, and all other aspects of the instrument. Special chapters are dedicated to reeds (selecting, testing, and adjusting reeds), mouthpieces and ligatures, and maintenance.

Tipbook Trumpet & Trombone, Flugelhorn & Cornet

The Tipbook on brass instruments focuses on the smaller horns listed in the title. It explains all jargon you come across when you're out to buy or rent an instrument, from bell material to the shape of the bore, the leadpipe, valves and valve slides, and all other elements of the horn. Mouthpieces, a crucial choice for the sound and playability of all brasswinds, are covered in a separate chapter.

Tipbook Keyboard & Digital Piano

Buying a home keyboard or a digital piano may find you confronted with numerous unfamiliar terms. *Tipbook Keyboard & Digital Piano* explains all of them in a very easy-to-read fashion — from hammer action and non-weighted keys to MIDI, layers and splits, arpeggiators and sequencers, expression

233

pedals and multi-switches, and more, including special chapters on how to judge the instrument's sound, accompaniment systems, and the various types of connections these instruments offer.

Tipbook Saxophone – The Complete Guide

At first glance, all alto saxophones look alike. And all tenor saxophones do too — yet they all play and sound different from each other. *Tipbook Saxophone* discusses the instrument in detail, explaining the key system and the use of additional keys, the different types of pads, corks, and springs, mouthpieces and how they influence timbre and playability, reeds (and how to select and adjust them) and much more.

Tipbook Buyer's Guide to the Saxophone

The Tipbook Buyer's Guide to the Saxophone focuses on the information you need to make an informed purchase of the instrument, a mouthpiece, reeds, and related products. Presented in a highly accessible format, with an easy-to-follow layout, and loaded with insider tips that help you understand your instrument. How does the alloy influence the sound of the instrument? Are extra keys helpful? What is the effect of a larger tip opening, a baffle, or a longer facing? How do you find your perfect reed? The Tipbook Buyer's Guide provides an answer to all these – and many more – questions!

Tipbook Vocals – The Singing Voice

Tipbook Vocals –The Singing Voice helps you realize the full potential of your singing voice. The book, written in close collaboration with classical and non-classical singers and teachers, allows you to discover the world's most personal and precious instrument without reminding you of anatomy class. Topics include breathing and breath support, singing loudly without hurting your voice, singing in tune, the timbre of your voice, articulation, registers and ranges, memorizing lyrics, and more. The main purpose of the dedicated chapter on voice care is to prevent negative symptoms.

Tipbook Amplifiers & Effects

Whether you need a guitar amp, a sound system, a multi-effects unit for a bass guitar, or a keyboard amplifier, *Tipbook Amplifiers & Effects* helps you make a good choice. Two chapters explain general features (controls, equalizers, speakers, MIDI, etc.) and figures (watts, ohms, impedance, etc.), and further chapters cover the specifics of guitar amps, bass amps, keyboard amps, acoustic amps, and sound systems. Effects and effect units are dealt with in detail, and there are dedicated chapters on microphones and pickups, and cables and wireless systems.

Tipbook Music for Kids and Teens – a Guide for Parents

How do you inspire children to play music? How do you inspire them to practice? What can you do to help them select an instrument, to reduce stage fright, or to practice effectively? What can you do to make practice fun? How do you reduce sound levels and prevent hearing damage? These and many more questions are dealt with in *Tipbook Music for Kids and Teens – a Guide for Parents and Caregivers*. The book addresses all subjects related to the musical education of children from pre-birth to pre-adulthood, covering phases of musical development, learning styles, instrument selection, assessing a music teacher, practicing, guidance and motivation, and much more.

International editions

The Tipbook Series is also available in Spanish, French, German, Dutch, Swedish, and (as of 2007) Chinese.

235

TIPBOOK SERIES
MUSIC AND MUSICAL
INSTRUMENTS

Tipbook Acoustic Guitar	*ISBN 90-76192-37-5*
Tipbook Amplifiers & Effects	*ISBN 90-76192-40-5*
Tipbook Cello	*ISBN 90-76192-47-2*
Tipbook Clarinet	*ISBN 90-76192-46 4*
Tipbook Drums – The Complete Guide	*ISBN 90-8767-102-4*
Tipbook Electric Guitar & Bass Guitar	*ISBN 90-76192-35-9*
Tipbook Flute & Piccolo	*ISBN 90-76192-42-1*
Tipbook Home Keyboard & Digital Piano	*ISBN 90-76192-31-6*
Tipbook Music for Kids and Teens	*ISBN 90-76192-50-2*
Tipbook Music on Paper	*ISBN 90-76192-32-4*
Tipbook Piano	*ISBN 90-76192-36-7*
Tipbook Saxophone – The Complete Guide	*ISBN 90-8767-101-6*
Tipbook Buyer's Guide to the Saxophone	*ISBN 90-8767-501-1*
Tipbook Trumpet & Trombone	*ISBN 90-76192-41-3*
Tipbook Violin & Viola	*ISBN 90-76192-39-1*
Tipbook Vocals	*ISBN 90-76192-38-3*

Check www.tipbook.com for additional information!